# Teaching pupils how to learn

**Bill Lucas**

**Toby Greany**

**Jill Rodd &**

**Ray Wicks**

research, practice and INSET resources

CAMPAIGN FOR **LEARNING**

Published by Network Educational Press Ltd
PO Box 635
Stafford
ST16 1BF

Editor: Martha Kürzl
Design and layout: Neil Hawkins
Mind maps pages 11–12: Philip Chambers, Learning Technologies Ltd
Printed by ColourBooks Ltd., Dublin, Ireland.

# Contents

## Understanding the theory

## Exploring the research findings

## Putting it into practice

# Foreword

The Campaign for Learning clearly shares this government's passion for learning. We can all gain from the broad and bold perspective adopted in this report.

Some of the ideas in the report are ones that the government, local education authorities and schools – in partnership – are already starting to put into practice in the classroom through the National Literacy, Numeracy and Key Stage 3 Strategies, for example. There must certainly be a greater emphasis in the classroom on explicit, engaging and expert teaching and learning. And I hope that, if the Campaign for Learning repeats its poll of pupils in a few years, far fewer will say they spend their time in class copying from the board or a book. Those sorts of dry lessons must become a thing of the past.

Other ideas in the report will stimulate and challenge our current practices at all levels: central and local government, and all types of educational institutions from early years to secondary schools, from colleges to universities and beyond. Whether the report's emerging recommendations are the way forward remains to be seen. But the Campaign for Learning is rightly challenging us all to think carefully about the education system the country needs for the 21st century.

Changing practice on such a large scale is a complex business, as we ourselves have learned from implementing our national strategies. Part of the key to success seems to be schools' own capacity to make sense of the wealth of resources and initiatives in their own local context. This puts the emphasis where it should be: on headteachers and teachers as powerful professionals, drawing together and making a reality of learning communities.

I commend this report of the first Phase of the 'learning to learn' research project to a wide audience of those concerned with learning, and look forward to the project's continuing work.


Stephen Timms
*Minister of State for School Standards*

# Foreword for the second edition

When we wrote *Teaching Pupils How to Learn* back in 2002 we based it on the findings from the first year of our research in 24 schools. Since then we have completed a further year of research with the original schools, which validated our original findings that using Learning to Learn approaches can help:

- Raise standards
- Enhance teacher morale
- Improve pupil motivation and confidence in learning.

You can read the detailed findings from the second year of the research and how our thinking developed over the course of the project in Creating a Learning to Learn School (Greany and Rodd, NEP, 2003).

Working with the project schools has been a fascinating and hugely rewarding experience and I am extremely grateful to them for all their ideas, enthusiasm and hard work. We are maintaining the network and most of the schools are still using and researching Learning to Learn, increasingly seeing it as central to all that they do.

In September 2003 we started a much larger three-year research project working with 34 schools in three geographical clusters and supported by the University of Newcastle Thinking Skills Research Centre. The research will look in more detail at the impact of using Learning to Learn approaches and the practicalities of doing so. We will publish annual research findings and hold regular conferences and events from Spring 2005 onwards.

Log onto the Campaign for Learning's website – www.campaignforlearning.org.uk and click on 'Learning through School' – for up-to-date information on the project, to attend our national conferences/events and to participate in ongoing online discussions about Learning to Learn.

Toby Greany
*Campaign for Learning*

December 2003

# Why 'learning to learn' is important

Understanding and implementing 'learning to learn' approaches in schools is a potential way forward.

We have all been participating in the Campaign for Learning's action research project and have seen real benefits as a consequence. In our experience standards rise, morale improves and pupils become more engaged. We urge all schools to explore the emerging theory which underpins this work and to consider introducing it themselves.

All schools today face challenges and many face additional constraints, such as teacher shortages, pupil disaffection and limited parental involvement and support. Clearly 'learning to learn' must be integrated with strategies on a range of fronts for it to achieve its potential in these circumstances, but we believe that by re-focusing teachers and pupils on the core purpose of education – namely learning – it offers a way forward for all schools.

Alan McMurdo
Prince William School

Richard Wallis
Sandwich Technology School

Steve Byatt
Ellowes Hall School

Jill Stuart
Summerhill School

Jen Cartwright
Ladysmith First School

S. F. Davies
Ogmore School

Dot Charlton
Hipsburn County First School

Elaine Wilmot
West Grove Primary School

Tony Downing
Campion School

David Hudson
King James's School

C Jones
Tasker Millward School

Jonathon de Sausmares
Henry Beaufort School

Derek Wise
Cramlington Community High School

Philip S Wood
Lytham St Anne's High School

Sheelagh Brown
Kingdown School

Ian Kenworthy
Camborne School and Community College

Tom Clark
George Spencer School

Michael Wood
Cornwallis School

Mary Royles (Joint acting head)
Tapton School

Sharron Colton
Ashgate Nursery School

Albyn Snowdon
Mortimer Comprehensive School

Sheila Ireland
Malet Lambert School

# About this book

*Teaching pupils how to learn* has been written to help schools put into practice some ideas about learning which, we believe, will help pupils to become more confident and effective learners. It includes the findings from the first Phase (September 2000 to July 2001) of the Campaign for Learning's national 'learning to learn' action research project, which has involved 24 schools covering all ages throughout England and Wales.

The book falls into three sections:

The first (chapters 1 and 2) explores some of the theory underpinning the idea of 'learning to learn'. It also describes some of the current policy framework into which any initiative in schools has to fit. Case studies illustrate some of the issues.

The second (chapters 3 to 5) outlines findings from the first Phase of the 'learning to learn' research project which started in England and Wales in 2000. These are analysed in the context of questions such as 'Can learning to learn raise standards?' In Chapter 5, a series of recommendations are set out for taking forward 'learning to learn' nationally. Again, case studies illustrate some of the issues.

The third and final section (chapters 6 and 7) offers some practical suggestions for individual schools wishing to take the idea of 'learning to learn' forward.

This book comes at the start of a journey. It lays out an early route map for anyone genuinely seeking to understand learning afresh in the light of new evidence, old prejudices and a fast changing world. The findings from the first Phase of the 'learning to learn' project are only tentative at this stage. Further research has now been completed, and interim outcomes are outlined in the follow up title *Creating a Learning to Learn School* (Network Educational Press, 2003)

# Acknowledgements

This book would not have been written without the dedicated help and support of many people and organizations. We are particularly grateful to our hard-working advisory board: John Abbott, Dr Javier Bajer, Sir Christopher Ball, Tom Bentley, Tony Buzan, Jose Chambers, Professor Guy Claxton, Galina Dolya, Maggie Farrah, Professor Ann Floyd, David Higgins, Dr Peter Honey, Jim Houghton, Lesley James, Professor Elizabeth Leo, Dr Juliet Merrifield, Roger Opie, Colin Rose, Judy Sebba, Alistair Smith, Lady Mary Tovey and Kate Williamson, and to our project patrons: Professor Tim Brighouse, Sir John Daniel, Professor Susan Greenfield and Professor David Hargreaves.

To our major sponsors, the Esmée Fairbairn Foundation, the Lifelong Learning Foundation, Accelerated Learning Systems Ltd and nferNelson, we are especially grateful, as we are to all those other organizations which have supported us along the way: Alite, Brain Trust, Comino Foundation, Design Council, National Grid plc, the University of the First Age, RSA, Celemi and, of course, our publishers, Network Educational Press. Pictures supplied from DfES and Impact Design & Marketing.

# 1 | What is 'learning to learn'?

## The nature of learning

It is easy to forget the fact that you are learning.

Perhaps this is because, from an early age, we learn how to walk and to talk without really being aware of it. Then we learn to read, write and use numbers from our parents and our teachers, again very much as part of growing up. And gradually we gain an understanding of the world about us and, of course, of ourselves as individuals within society. Much of this we do without knowing *how* we do it.

For most people there are key landmark moments in their learning: riding a bicycle without stabilizers, reading a first book, realizing that the sun comes up each day of the year, cooking a meal without any help from parents. There may even be times when they need specific support to overcome a difficulty or get to grips with something they find difficult. At such moments the learner becomes more conscious of the process, for example, when she or he is learning to drive a car and complex activities like pulling out into fast moving traffic have to be carefully sequenced.

At school our learning is organized into different content areas and, for the first time, is explicitly taught. Someone teaches us maths, English, science, history and so on, with each subject having a different set of rules and processes to learn. So, maths teachers teach us how to do simple adding and subtracting before moving on to complex multiplication or division, at each stage explaining how these things are done.

The introduction of the national curriculum has meant that all pupils are taught broadly the same content in each subject area, but this has only served to reinforce an emphasis on *what* you learn rather than *how* you learn it. This is less true in the core areas of literacy and numeracy since the introduction of the national strategies, which have helped teachers make the process of acquiring these skills more explicit. Thus, the Literacy Hour in primary schools aims to give pupils a sound conceptual grasp of words, grammar and structures in order to understand how language functions. At Key Stage 3, the strategy involves looking across subjects to highlight how their writing conventions differ, for example, how a science experiment write up differs from an English essay.

In most areas, however, teachers must focus so relentlessly on covering the curriculum that they have little time to consider how best they might do it to meet the differing needs of the pupils in their class or to help their pupils understand why and how they are learning things. As a result, those pupils who manage to remain motivated generally see learning as a process of remembering and regurgitating facts for the purpose of carrying on 'learning' at the next stage (that is, college or university), with the end result being to 'get a good job' when, by implication, learning can cease. Far too few pupils leave school with a developed understanding of themselves as learners or of how or why they should carry on learning throughout life.

# Learning how to learn

Are there, in fact, some things that teachers can do that will encourage learning and some which may have an adverse affect? Should we teach pupils how to learn or do we assume that they will acquire this capability by osmosis? Is such a thing even possible or is learning too context specific for 'learning to learn' to have any meaning? Is 'learning to learn' just a fancy synonym for study skills? Or is there a learning 'grammar' that children can learn in order to make them successful learners in school and throughout life?

It was a series of questions like this that led the Campaign for Learning (CfL) to bring together an alliance of individuals and organizations in 2000 to develop a research project – outlined in section 2 of this book – to seek some of the answers. Our hypothesis is that you can teach pupils how to learn more effectively and that 'learning to learn' is, therefore, a meaningful concept in schools.

# The elements of 'learning to learn'

'Learning to learn' is hard to define. This is the working definition we developed for the research project outlined in this book:

'Learning to learn' is a process of discovery about learning. It involves a set of principles and skills which, if understood and used, help learners learn more effectively and so become learners for life. At its heart is the belief that learning is learnable.

'Learning to learn' is essentially about the process of learning. It involves understanding the kind of strategies that effective learners need to develop to become autonomous. To do this it inevitably involves meta-cognition or meta-learning – the development of a language to describe thinking and learning processes. We are only too aware that by using words like these we run the risk of putting people off. But it is equally clear to us that having an evidence-based and robust methodology is very important. One of the challenges for us is to develop an accessible language to help learners and teachers talk about learning as easily as if they were using technical terms such as 'metaphor' to talk about a poem or a story.

The mind maps on the next two pages give an indication of some of the elements in visual terms. The first one was our starting point. The second emerged from a meeting of the project schools at the end of the first year. These maps only give a snapshot of our thinking about the elements involved in 'learning to learn', and already this has moved on, as you will see from the following pages which aim to outline the process, principles and emerging theory underpinning 'learning to learn'.

## Mind map developed at the start of the 'Learning to Learn' Project to describe the elements involved

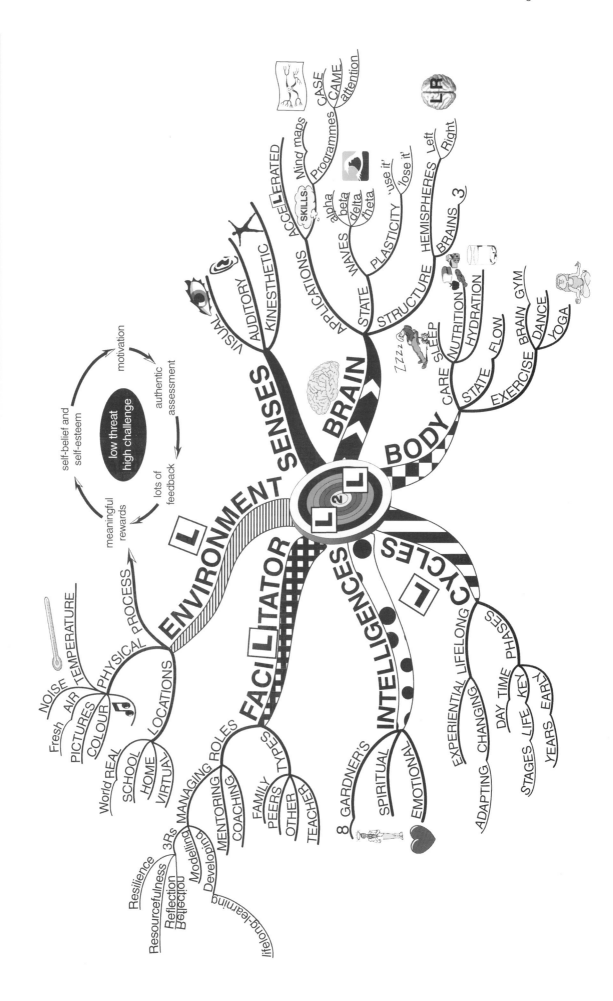

## Mind map developed at the end of the first Phase of the 'Learning to Learn' Project to describe interim achievements

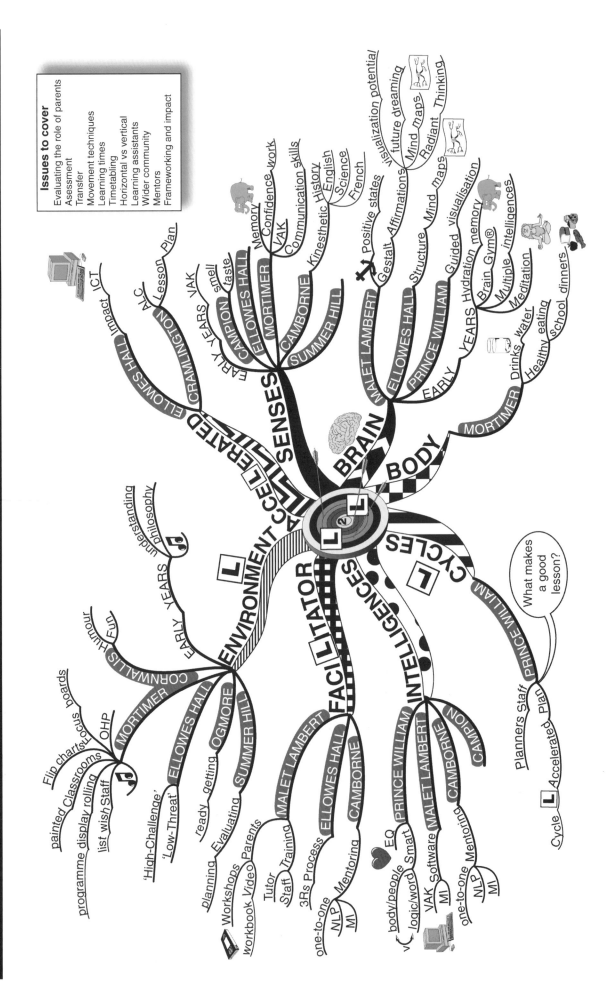

**Issues to cover**
Evaluating the role of parents
Asessment
Transfer
Movement techniques
Learning times
Timetabling
Horizontal vs vertical
Learning assistants
Wider community
Mentors
Frameworking and impact

# Creating a 'learning to learn' school

## Cramlington Community High School

### Aim

To assess the results of creating a 'learning to learn' school.

### Process

- INSET from expert presenters to provide stimulus for change and to encourage staff to experiment and question the status quo.

- Headteacher becomes 'head learner'.

- Address concerns of staff. Combine idealism with realism.

- Include in the School Development Plan and publish specific action plans and timescales.

- Introduce accelerated learning lesson planning framework (see Case study on page 54) and train staff further to use this and apply its approaches in the classroom.

- Physical environment changed to clear 'dead' space and introduce learning zones (reading, doing, discussion) and more visual/learning materials.

- Introduce flexible timetabling, for example through double periods, to enable a variety of teaching and learning strategies.

- New initiatives such as performance management and ICT aligned to 'learning to learn' strategies.

### Outcomes

- Teachers report student motivation improved and positive response from pupils confirmed by questionnaires.

- Staff report feeling 'revitalized' – 'accelerated learning has played an important part in making us think about learning and as a result we are teaching more effectively, our lessons are more engaging and pupils want to be in them.

- Ofsted confirmed, 'the open, creative discourse encouraged among the school's staff has resulted in thoughtful and searching exploration of what makes students learn effectively. Staff share new ideas from research, conferences and courses and discuss the teaching of their subject with rigour and imagination. As a result much of the teaching is fresh and innovative in approach'.

- The headteacher, Derek Wise, and Mark Lovatt, Head of Science, have written Creating An Accelerated Learning School.

Learning points

- Introducing new learning methods takes careful planning, sustained enthusiasm and sensitivity.

- Achieving culture change among staff is facilitated by clear buy-in from the head and an overall structure and lesson planning framework that allows teachers to apply approaches consistently but flexibly.

- The purpose of lessons is not to 'do' multiple intelligences or VAK (visual, auditory and kinesthetic), but to achieve learning outcomes by 'knowing the pupils and being sensitive to their learning needs'.

# The theoretical background

The conceptual basis for 'learning to learn' draws on work from a wide range of different disciplines. These include cognitive neuroscience, learning and intelligence, motivational psychology and emotional intelligence. Specific writers, thinkers and researchers whose work has influenced the project's thinking include John Abbott, Philip Adey, Christopher Ball, Tom Bentley, Paul Black, Colin Blakemore, Tony Buzan, Guy Claxton, Edward de Bono, Reuven Feuerstein, Howard Gardner, Daniel Goleman, Susan Greenfield, Carla Hannaford, Trevor Hawes, John Holt, Mike Hughes, Eric Jensen, Elizabeth Leo, Colin Rose, Alistair Smith and Dylan Wiliam.

# The idea of learnacy and learnability

The key principle underpinning the project is that learning is learnable, and that individual learning dispositions can be developed. It was Guy Claxton who first began to talk of learnacy as a synonym for the area of expertise covered by the phrase 'learning to learn', and we have developed this further. What literacy is to reading, so learnacy is to learning.

Learnacy is the ability of learners to understand and apply strategies for improving their own learning. The word, is, of course, fraught with difficulties, as anyone who is good at it would presumably be a 'learnatic'! But then it was only in the 1990s that the extremely inelegant word 'numeracy' began to catch on.

It is widely accepted that all learners are born with a starter kit of reflexes, rudimentary maps and crude sets of responses. But we are less clear about how they go on to build an integrated set of more refined learning tools. What does seem to be the case is that we each develop preferred ways of doing things and that what works for one person may not be so helpful to someone else.

Neurological research evidence from Susan Greenfield and others indicates that the brain is programmed to tune itself in response to experience. All learners are unique in the way their brain has tuned itself in response to their own experience. Although a range of developmental factors influence learning, it appears that the natural learning ability of the brain can either be augmented or diminished as a result of the learner's experience.

The Campaign for Learning definition of learning is 'a process of active engagement with experience that may involve an increase in skills, knowledge, understanding, a deepening of values or the capacity to reflect. Effective learning leads to change, development and a desire to know more.'

There is often a certain randomness about learning. In fact, it can be a gamble, dependent on a whole range of factors. This is inevitable in an ever-changing world; however, we believe that learners could be helped to develop positive learning dispositions and become better equipped to manage their learning more effectively.

The following sections divide the key components of learnacy into four areas:

**A** The need for an explicit model of learning

**B** The concept of multiple intelligence

**C** The development of learning dispositions

**D** An understanding of the mind's operating systems.

These emerging concepts are presented as a scaffold for thinking and dialogue about teaching and learning in schools and elsewhere.

# A A model of learning

We have already explained that 'learning to learn' has at its core the idea that learning – like reading or dancing or running meetings – is learnable. Equally central is the fact that learning is a process and that there are some key aspects of this process which frequently get overlooked in schools.

In *Learning to learn: setting the agenda for schools in the 21st century*, the publication which initially set out the 'learning to learn' project, we presented the following model of learning as a way of helping teachers and pupils think about the learning process:

- Being ready to learn
- Being able to set and achieve goals
- Knowing how to learn best
- Harnessing creativity
- Being able to reflect, adapt and change.

This model can be summarized even more simply as 'Ready, Go, Steady', indicating three main stages to learning: 'before', 'during' and 'after'. These three stages are set out overleaf, with the kinds of questions that each one raises for learners.

| Ready | Being ready to learn<br><br>Being able to set and achieve goals | How can we manage our emotional state so that we are ready to learn? How much self-esteem do we need to have? Do we need to connect ourselves to and engage fully in the learning we are being offered? What do we need to know about motivation and how to motivate ourselves to learn? What kinds of intrinsic and extrinsic rewards work? How do we reduce our learning to manageable chunks? |
|---|---|---|
| Go | Knowing how to learn best<br><br>Harnessing creativity | How many different strategies do we have? Do we have the capacity to keep on learning when things get tough? What do we know about our own preferred learning styles and about how we like to take in data? Do we understand how our memory works? Do we have a model of a typical learning cycle? Are we in touch with our feelings? How do we use electronic media? Can we tolerate reasonable amounts of confusion, frustration and even uncertainty in our learning? Do we know how to ask questions and when to seek help? Do we assume that we have many intelligences? Are we able to listen to our hunches? Do we have strategies for thinking different thoughts and solving difficult problems? |
| Steady | Being able to reflect, adapt and change | How do we know how we are progressing? What is our attitude to making mistakes? Do we do things differently as a result of what we have learned? Do we know how to give and receive feedback? How well do we recognize what we have learned informally? |

An underlying assumption of this model, and hence the deliberate move away from the natural order of 'Ready, Steady, Go', is that we need to focus more on the before and after rather than on the middle bit.

There is plenty of good evidence that you cannot learn if you are not emotionally and psychologically ready for it. Put crudely, you cannot learn with an empty belly or with your self-esteem in tatters. Even if these factors are in place, you still need to be motivated to learn effectively. Indeed, even in apparently smoothly run classes, many pupils may be playing intellectual truant if they have not been engaged.

The implications for teachers of getting pupils ready to learn would include the development of approaches that

- Recognize where pupils are coming from, for example in terms of their self-esteem or any issues outside school, and help pupils prepare themselves for the learning in hand.

- Focus pupils' attention on the importance of factors such as diet, water, exercise, sleep and additives on learning effectiveness.

- Help pupils connect to their learning by relating it to their practical life experience.

In terms of the 'Go' stage, teachers can help pupils by recognizing and responding to individual differences in the ways that they learn. For example, given that learners have different preferences for how they take in information, teachers should present it visually, auditorily and kinesthetically (VAK) wherever possible. Equally, as the following section makes clear, teachers must recognize and respond to different forms of intelligence.

Finally, in the 'Steady' stage, unless you reflect on learning undertaken, you will never change. For learners to be able to adapt and take responsibility for their own learning they need to be offered formative (rather than just summative) assessment, as outlined by Paul Black and Dylan Wiliam and the Assessment Reform Group.

At each of these stages there are important implications for the learning environment that schools must provide. This must be:

- challenging

- not too threatening

- full of opportunities for giving and receiving feedback.

Equally, in terms of the learning environment and the fact that learning is largely a social activity, good schools work hard in a range of areas to create a reinforcing learning culture, for example by:

- Offering relevant learning opportunities for pupils outside the classroom.

- Providing positive opportunities for teachers to learn and share ideas and practice.

- Providing learning leadership.

- Working with parents and the wider community to provide learning role models.

Of course, 'Ready, Go, Steady' is not the only model of learning in use, or necessarily the best one. It takes its place in a long queue that starts with Jean Piaget and encompasses many others including David Kolb and Klas Mellander. Several schools used versions of the accelerated learning cycle developed by Alistair Smith:

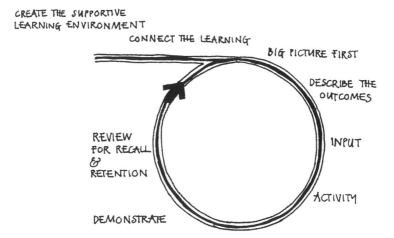

To develop a 'learning to learn' approach the important issue is, first of all, that teachers and learners have an explicit model and, secondly, that they actually use it. The impact of this can be seen from the case study on pages 54–55.

In conclusion, if we are to learn how to learn, we need to have a clear model of how learning takes place – the stages that we go through in order to learn effectively. Additional important elements in our conception of 'learning to learn' concern the nature of intelligence, the dispositions of the learner and the operating principles of the mind.

case
study

# Structuring teaching to preferred learning styles

## Camborne School and Community College – Year 8

### Aim

To assess the impact on learning resulting from structured lessons that reflect the preferred learning style of pupils.

### Process

Two mixed ability groups were involved in a series of poetry lessons as part of their English syllabus. The research group was identified as having preferred styles of three auditory, nine visual and 13 kinesthetic. The control group had seven visual and 14 kinesthetic.

The control group received 'traditional' lessons, while the following lesson structure was used for the research group:

1.  Being ready to learn

    Warm-up exercises involving moving around the room and working in pairs/small groups setting the scene/genre.

2.  Being able to set and achieve goals

    Aims were identified and a plan for the lesson that contained units of work each no longer than 15 minutes was outlined.

3.  Knowing how you learn best

    Pupils had previously filled in questionnaires and had a lesson covering preferred learning styles.

4.  Knowing how to be creative

    The study of poetry included predominantly kinesthetic activities:

    ■ Imagery

    ■ Moving to the 'rhythm' of the poem and number of syllables

    ■ Drama (context and content)

    ■ Discussion in pairs/groups

    ■ Emotional responses to characters and content

5.  Reflecting/adapting/changing

    Sum up the poem, what has been learned about the content, the emotions expressed and the sentences. Summarize key points with a mind map if appropriate.

Outcomes

■ Significant preference for kinesthetic learning in both research and control group.

■ Even in a subject with a natural focus on (auditory) language it is possible to create engaging and effective kinesthetic learning activities.

■ As the kinesthetic work developed pupils became less concerned with being right and more concerned with exploring the text.

■ Using a predominantly kinesthetic teaching style did enhance learning as well as the interest of pupils. In EN2 assessments the research group gained higher results than the control group and higher than would be predicted from earlier national curriculum tests scores.

Learning points

■ A structure to lessons that reflects how pupils learn best will bring results in both attainment and understanding.

■ Time should be spent at the beginning of each lesson to get pupils ready for learning and preferably into a state of 'curiosity'.

■ Confidence increases where a culture of creativity is encouraged and respect for how pupils work through their learning to arrive at solutions.

# B The concept of multiple intelligence

For too long IQ (Intellectual Quotient) has been the prevailing influence on theories of intelligence. It has made a single test the defining factor in whether or not someone sees themselves as 'intelligent'. But this has artificially inflated the importance of language and figures and taken little account of creativity, common sense or the ability to manage emotions.

In reality we know that intelligence involves a combination of know-how as well as know-what across a multitude of contexts. Psychologist Professor Howard Gardner started a welcome revolution here when he first developed the idea of multiple intelligences.

In the 1980s he started with seven, then introduced an eighth and is now toying with a ninth, existential intelligence. We think that there may be as many as ten: linguistic, mathematical, visual, physical, musical, environmental, emotional, social, physical and spiritual.

But the point is that there is more to life than IQ for anyone investigating the concept of 'learning to learn'.

# C The development of learning dispositions

Once we spoke about the three Rs of wRiting, Reading and aRithmetic. These were sensible words to use to describe the basic skills that, even today, remain the foundation for life. But in the modern world we need to develop an additional five Rs to be effective learners. Rather than being areas of knowledge and skill they are perhaps best described as 'attributes' or 'dispositions'.

If we look at what defines an effective lifelong learner, as Guy Claxton and his colleagues at Bristol University have begun to do, the following five dispositions seem to be of particular relevance:

1. Resilience (important in the Ready and Go stages)

2. Resourcefulness (important in the Ready and Go stages)

3. Remembering (important in the Go stage)

4. Reflectiveness (important in the Steady stage)

5. Responsiveness (important in the Steady stage).

A Resilient learner is one who can motivate herself and pick herself up and have another go on experiencing a knock back. A Resourceful learner knows how they learn best and how to set about their learning and draw on different sources of help. And so on.

Where teachers invest time in nurturing such dispositions, our belief is that pupils become more effective learners.

- Resilience can be built up when pupils acquire techniques for dealing with getting stuck; for example, by brainstorming five ways of tackling the feeling of mental blankness that hits them when they first see a difficult exam question or agreeing 'Ten things to do when I get stuck'.

- To encourage Resourcefulness, a teacher might give pupils structured opportunities to plan and manage their own learning, using different information resources.

- Remembering might be improved by learning recall strategies involving acronyms or rhymes.

- Peer assessment, oral and written, is one way of developing Reflectiveness.

- Responsiveness can be learned by pupils imitating a teacher who constantly adapts her behaviour in the light of changing situations and tells the class why she is doing so and why they might do similarly!

case
study

# Involving pupils in establishing the learning 'rules'

## Hipsburn First School – Years 1–3

### Aim

To engage pupils in exploring factors that help them learn.

### Process

All pupils in the school had previously worked with the teacher to understand their own preferred learning style.

Pupils worked in small groups of 4/5 thinking of times when they learned something new, enjoyable and interesting. The examples were written on cards and then sorted into themes. The themes were discussed and a collective agreement on the factors that helped the pupils learn was arrived at.

### Outcomes

The school implemented many of the ideas that the pupils felt helped them learn, which included:

- Knowing what they are going to be doing.
- Accepting that learning sometimes involves making mistakes.
- Being given credit for trying and taking risks.
- Varying the seating, sometimes sitting in a circle so they could discuss ideas.
- Sometimes working in silence and sometimes with gentle music to help them concentrate.
- Using music for a break.
- Doing Brain Gym® to keep our minds fresh.
- Drinking plenty of water.
- Feeling 'safe'.
- Discussing possibilities and opinions.
- Learning through the senses (seeing, listening and doing).
- Trying to understand their own strengths so we can use them.
- Learning from each other.

Evidence gathered following the introduction of these learning 'rules' shows that the children enjoy learning in an environment they helped 'create'. The school has since gained recognition from the DfES, winning an 'Excellence Award', which further endorsed the impact of the pupil/teacher relationship.

Learning points

■ Pupils at a young age understand what helps them learn and are capable of taking the responsibility that 'empowerment' brings.

■ Learning is greatly enhanced by understanding how pupils learn and providing a supporting environment and 'ethos'.

■ Understanding how pupils learn is key.

# D Understanding how the mind works

Little or no time is spent during teacher training on understanding the key operating principles of the mind. Yet there is growing evidence from cognitive neuroscience indicating that the brain's innumerable functions can all impact upon how we learn.

When teachers understand how the brain works and some of its critical functions, they are more able to capitalize on the brain's natural functions and processes in their approaches to teaching and therefore improve learning effectiveness.

Five of the key operating principles of the mind that teachers need to address in their teaching are:

1. Exploration (the mind's capacity to continually develop and harness creativity by endlessly exploring)

2. Connection (the mind's disposition for making connections in different domains)

3. Pattern making (the mind's disposition for looking for and creating patterns)

4. Imitation (the mind's love of modelling what it sees)

5. Balancing stress and challenge (the impact of combinations of stress and challenge on learning and performance).

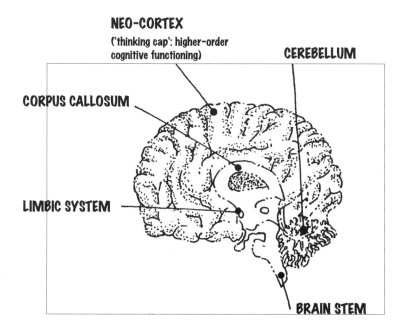

We know that, while there is much research and common sense wisdom about how learners learn already in the public domain, there is much more to find out. With the amazing developments in cognitive neuroscience taking place at the moment, we are discovering new things every year.

At one time we thought that the Earth was flat. About 150 years ago, we thought that there were distinctly separate parts of the brain that dealt with different functions. We now have much more rounded solutions that invite a new complexity of response.

# Conclusion: ASK not KSA

The elements of 'learning to learn' outlined here lead to an inevitable conclusion about what is important in schools. In the last two decades of the 20th century, following the introduction of the national curriculum, success has increasingly been defined by subject Knowledge (measured through exam league tables). Skills are seen as important and Attitudes to learning less so. This is the KSA world that dominates formal schooling.

If you believe in 'learning to learn' then you are likely to want to reverse these priorities. You will prefer an ASK approach, where Attitudes – we might even say Attributes – are most important, then Skills and last of all Knowledge.

It is an irony that the 21st century in referred to as the Knowledge or Information Age when assessment criteria still demand that students accumulate large quantities of knowledge in order to pass examinations. It is our contention that to deal with a surfeit of knowledge, effective learners need certain attributes and their associated skills. They can get the information as they need it.

Knowledge is important. Indeed you cannot see complex patterns and inter-relationships between elements without it. Nor can you determine what is subtle and original if you have little knowledge. But if teachers want to help pupils become effective learners, we have no doubt that their focus should be on developing attributes rather than acquiring knowledge.

Teaching becomes a means of creating and supporting a learning culture in a school and much less of the transmitting of information and skills. The baton is passed to the pupil to become an independent learner in the race against time for success. Rather than relying on the teachers, pupils need to be more reliant on each other.

# A new pedagogy

'Learning to learn' is emerging as a new pedagogy that has specific implications for teachers and teaching approaches. The intention of the 'learning to learn' project is to develop an evidence-base for teachers that integrates emerging theoretical knowledge with research evidence from the classroom.

There is certainly an emerging underpinning to the idea of 'learning to learn'. The resources listed on page 77 provide more opportunities for these to be explored and the testimony of schools in the second section is beginning to provide some of the evidence.

As Carl Rogers put it in *Freedom to Learn*:

'Teaching and imparting of knowledge made sense in an unchanging environment. This is why it has been an unquestioned function for centuries. But if there is one truth about modern man, it is that he lives in an environment that is continually changing.

'The only man who is educated is the man who has learned how to adapt and change; the man who has realized that no knowledge is secure, that only the process of seeking knowledge gives a basis of security.'

# 2 | Why is 'learning to learn' relevant today?

## Life in the 21st century

Underpinning the 'learning to learn' project is a belief that the excluded of the 21st century will be those who do not know how to learn. In the past it was considered perfectly normal to leave school at 16 and consider one's 'learning' to be over. The majority of men expected to go into blue-collar jobs that had changed little since their fathers' day, while the majority of women expected to stay at home and raise a family. Only 2 or 3 per cent of school leavers went to university.

Today, this picture seems a distant memory. In the workplace, 'jobs for life' have disappeared, women outnumber men and new technologies are transforming the way we work.

These changes are inextricably linked to wider changes in the global economy. Faced by increased competition from emerging economies where labour is cheap, the UK's economy has shifted from large-scale manufacturing to high-tech industries, such as aerospace and pharmaceuticals, and value-added services. Meanwhile, technological advances in computers and the internet have impacted hugely on traditional ways of working. Whereas in the past vast numbers of jobs did not require even basic literacy skills, today the vast majority involve intermediate or advanced skills.

Old industries (and many venerable British companies) have disappeared, while new ones are constantly emerging. Value has been transformed, even after the crash of the dot com bubble. Low-cost airline Ryanair is worth as much on the stock exchange today as British Airways. The need to keep up with international competition is relentless. But our productivity rates are among the lowest in Europe, meaning that we have to work the longest hours just to remain competitive.

## Learning to keep afloat

So today the UK's prosperity increasingly depends on the brains, not the brawn, of its citizens. We experience this in any number of different ways, from the regular need to update our computer skills, to the subtle shifts in organizational structure which have replaced hierarchies with 'self-managed teams', networks and homeworkers.

Meanwhile, we are faced by an array of social, ecological and political transformations that require sophisticated collective action. From violent crime to race riots, from suicide bombers to the 'death of democracy', from third world poverty to global warming, the issues threaten to overwhelm us as never before.

In our personal lives, we struggle to define our own identities. Family structures are becoming more fluid. We increasingly define ourselves according to a shifting set of identities that might include anything from our race, gender, sexuality or religious beliefs, to our shopping or television-watching preferences.

Change is endemic all around us and, while many people thrive in this fast-paced information-packed environment, others struggle to keep up. The simple difference between those that sink and those that swim is learning. It is not coincidental that huge numbers of those in prison have poor basic skills or that those with university degrees earn exponentially more than the unqualified over the course of their lifetimes.

The evidence is clear: people with few skills are at ever greater risk of social and economic exclusion. We must learn not just to keep up, but to stay on top of life in the 21st century. But this is about far more than just individual success: the relentless individualism and consumerism of our media age requires thoughtful learning for both personal fulfilment and collective citizenship.

# Education, education, education

In response to these challenges, the government has committed itself to raising standards in schools, persuading young people to stay on in education past 16, and working to raise the skill levels of adults.

Since 1997 it has introduced many initiatives covering every aspect of education, from Sure Start programmes and enhanced early years provision, through to the National Literacy and Numeracy Strategies, the Key Stage 3 strategy and Curriculum 2000 in schools. Within the lifelong learning arena, we have seen the creation of the Learning and Skills Council and learndirect and initiatives such as the adult basic skills strategy and the target for 50 per cent of under-30s to be entering higher education by 2010.

The reforms in schools are aimed at ensuring high standards for all and, increasingly, tailoring learning and broadening choice for individual pupils as they develop. They have been accompanied by parallel investments in professional development for teachers, for example through the new National College for School Leadership and the creation of Advanced Skills Teachers and Beacon Schools. This is seen as part of a wider 'modernization of the teaching profession', for example through linking pay to performance.

The approach has seen considerable success and, despite the levelling off in achievement indicated by the 2001 results, the government is considering even higher targets of 85 per cent of 11 year olds achieving level 4 in English and maths, and 35 per cent achieving level 5 by 2004.

Of course, one of the major subtexts to these initiatives and improvements is the stress that they have put on teachers and schools. The Department for Education and Skills is increasingly coming to recognize that teacher recruitment and retention is perhaps its greatest challenge and that failure to improve morale in the profession could scupper its efforts to raise standards. This has led to above inflation pay rises, golden handshakes and training salaries for new teachers as well as a major review of workload and bureaucracy. However, despite some successes in increasing recruitment, major criticisms from existing teachers who feel disempowered by centralized reforms and a lack of professional autonomy have yet to be seriously addressed.

Another key question is whether the reforms will support those most at risk of social exclusion to fulfil their potential. There is no doubt that the government is committed to this, and reforms such as Sure Start, Excellence in Cities and the ConneXions service are specifically aimed at meeting this objective. But still, while 80 per cent of young people from Social Class 1 professional families enter Higher Education today, just 14 per cent of those from Social Class 5 do. Greater support will yet be needed. Perhaps we will also need to test out more imaginative approaches to defining a curriculum for all.

case
study

# Brain-based mentoring

## Camborne School and Community College – Year 11

Aim

To re-energize pupils to fulfil their learning capability.

Process

Eighteen pupils who achieved level 5 in each of their KS3 national curriculum tests were chosen for 1:1 mentoring.

Mentor sessions took place in school time with pupils released from lessons for 45-minute sessions. Parents agreed and took an active interest.

Pupils had absolute freedom to talk openly with information only passed on with their consent. Pupils were free to leave the programme if they felt it was not giving value and were expected to keep records of their activities in the form of a study log.

### Session 1

- Likes and dislikes. Highs and lows.
- Times of optimism/pessimism.
- 'Dreaming' of what the future holds and relating back to present action.

### Session 2

- Identifying and analysing the implications of preferred learning style and multiple intelligence profile.
- Report produced for pupil/parent shared (with agreement) with their teachers.

### Session 3

- Exploring brain-based learning strategies based on session 2 findings (for example, mind maps, study-buddy, flashcards, and so on).
- Examination and charting of time management through use of study logs.

### Session 4

- Pupils take apart and reconstruct their week around how they learn best and intersperse exercise, leisure time and review periods.
- Chart becomes framework for the future and is shared with parents.

Sessions all start with reviews. Four sessions were generally sufficient although a few pupils had extra sessions that encompassed challenging self-limiting beliefs, negative expectations and study skills.

Outcomes

- 94 per cent of pupils felt the mentoring had helped.
- 88 per cent of parents had noticed a significant positive change in their child's attitude to school work.
- 50 per cent of pupils exceeded statistical expectations in their GCSEs.

Feedback from the teachers included:

'Ria and Sarah have clearly benefited from the mentoring sessions. Their attitude to lessons, style in which they take notes (mind maps, bullet points, and so on) and their openness to try the various teaching and learning styles has been brilliant. Wouldn't it be great if you had time to mentor every child throughout the school? I hope that this programme continues and expands.'

'RA got a C in her mocks and has a strong C for coursework. We've now set some targets based on her results and I'm confident she will do well. ML got a C in her mocks and should get a B in May. They are getting more confident all the time. Things look promising. Cheers.'

Learning points

- Understanding how pupils learn and developing learning strategies is a vital part of maximizing potential.
- Teachers, parents and pupils working together is a powerful combination.
- Self-esteem and positive self-image are important pre-requisites.

# Towards the school of the future?

So where is the government's education strategy heading? In the short-to-medium term the targets described above and others like them clearly indicate that raising standards will rightly remain the driving imperative. But how will this be done? Through more of the same or a different approach?

As the Secretary of State for Education and Skills, Estelle Morris took some important steps towards creating a more radical vision of the future of schooling. She dared to suggest that teachers may increasingly become the managers of learning, working with a range of para-professionals such as teaching assistants, to develop and deliver individualized learning for every pupil. She also launched *Transforming the way we learn: a vision for the future of ICT in schools*, which sets out how e-learning could be blended with existing provision to create the 21st-century classroom. These kinds of approaches are currently being piloted in 30 schools around the country.

*Transforming the way we learn* sets out the following skills needed by teachers in delivering effective e-learning:

- Judging when ICT is the appropriate tool for a particular task and when it isn't, and integrating such opportunities into their teaching as with any other educational tool.

- Being liberated from the traditional role as the fount of all knowledge so that they have more opportunities to innovate and provide the spark that stimulates achievement and creativity in their pupils.

- Working with pupils to agree and manage personalized learning programmes, including the provision of support and guidance (for example in relation to the choice of an appropriate range of traditional and digital learning resources).

- Agreeing targets that are informed by better benchmarking material and the ability to track the progress of individuals and groups of pupils.

- Appreciating the implications of learning that takes place outside of school and exploiting such opportunities to the full.

- Effectively utilizing the availability of learning assistants and mentoring programmes (involving learning mentors and pupils themselves).

There is much to cheer about here that would sit very comfortably within a 'learning to learn' approach. Yet, despite its refreshing breadth and vision, *Transforming the way we learn* only serves to emphasize the absence of a unifying theory or definition of learning at the heart of the government's education strategy. It is right in recognizing that no amount of technology will reduce the need for teachers to facilitate effective learning, but unless teachers are freed up from covering curriculum content and pupils are freed from relentless summative assessment, then standards will mean little beyond the ability of both sides to play the learning game.

This is not to say that the government is not aware of the need for education to develop a broader set of skills and attitudes than those assessed by national curriculum tests and GCSEs. This can be seen in support for out-of-school hours learning, the new citizenship curriculum, learning mentors and community schooling approaches, to name just a few initiatives.

Equally, aware that employers require more vocational skills and that too many school leavers lack basic employability and work readiness skills, the government is working hard to enhance the vocational pathway versus the traditional academic route. This can be seen in the introduction of new vocational qualifications and a broader curriculum with greater choice post-14 as well as a review of education-business links and work placements.

Yet the truth is that for most pupils the classroom of today is remarkably similar to traditional classrooms experienced throughout the 20th century. This can be seen in the responses of 2000 pupils (all pupils 11–16) to the question overleaf, when asked by MORI on behalf of the Campaign for Learning in 2000:

Which three of the following do you do most often in class?

| | |
|---|---|
| Copy from the board or a book | 56% |
| Have a class discussion | 37% |
| Listen to a teacher talking for a long time | 37% |
| Take notes while my teacher talks | 26% |
| Work in small groups to solve a problem | 25% |
| Spend time thinking quietly on my own | 22% |
| Talk about my work with a teacher | 22% |
| Work on a computer | 12% |
| Learn things that relate to the real world | 11% |

*(2000 pupils, 11-16 Years, MORI 2000)*

Sadly, when MORI asked another group of pupils the same question in 2002 the situation had barely changed.

Which three of the following do you do most often in class?

| | |
|---|---|
| Copy from the board or a book | 63% |
| Listen to a teacher talking for a long time | 37% |
| Have a class discussion | 31% |
| Spend time thinking quietly on my own | 24% |
| Work in small groups to solve a problem | 22% |
| Take notes while my teacher talks | 20% |
| Talk about my work with a teacher | 16% |
| Learn things that relate to the real world | 12% |
| Work on a computer | 10% |

*(2670 pupils, 11-16 Years, MORI 2002)*

case
study

# Parents and children working together

## Malet Lambert School

### Aim

To assess how parental understanding of L2L can help in supporting pupils fulfil their potential.

### Process

Project in collaboration with local primary schools and the University of Lincolnshire and Humberside:

■ 55 volunteer parents enrolled on a six-week L2L course.

■ Course was largely IT based containing input on understanding learning, learning styles and multiple intelligences.

■ Facilitated sessions included reflection and analysis of past learning experiences and parents' role in educating children.

### Outputs

■ Of 55 parents enrolled, 49 completed programme and gained Higher Education accreditation (6 CAT points at Level 1).

■ 46 reported that the course had helped tremendously in improving confidence in working with their children to support the school's use of 'learning to learn' methods.

Comments included: 'I find it hard to learn, but now I understand about how I learn best, I can make sure I do it in a way that suits me. I didn't learn much at school because it didn't suit me and the way I learn.'

'I actually enjoy helping my child to learn...I thought I had to have all the answers, which I knew I didn't have. But now I know how to help them in other ways, it's great!'

■ One headteacher reported 'parents are becoming more involved in supporting their children using multisensory teaching methods'.

■ Schools reported that parents were more aware of the optimal conditions for learning which they were able to apply to home-based learning.

■ Pupils' feedback was very positive largely around having parents that understand what they are doing.

### Learning points

■ Parents need a similar understanding of the 'how' to learn if they are to support their child's learning and be consistent with the approach taken by schools.

■ Learning at home based on an understanding of learning preferences and multisensory input can help enhance potential and provide motivation.

■ Schools have a responsibility to help parents understand how they are working to fulfil pupils' learning potential.

■ The payback of having informed parents working on a collaborative basis is compelling.

# What about 'learning, learning, learning'?

Of course, the MORI findings on page 30 by no means reflect the practice of all teachers. Good teachers have always known how to motivate pupils, present information in a variety of engaging ways and ensure that real learning takes place in the classroom.

But, equally, the narrow focus of most initial teacher training and ongoing support for teachers, coupled with the huge pressures on them to maintain discipline, 'cover' the curriculum and achieve results, prevents many others from doing so. Currently, in the drive to raise standards, pupils must sit as passengers and learning takes a back seat.

The excellent and essential work done by schools and teachers to raise standards and provide all children with the basics of literacy and numeracy is to be commended. But simply working harder to raise standards along the same lines will only produce ever more teacher overload and burn-out. The level 3 or D-grade pupils just capable of reaching the target will be dragged up to the line, while the remainder are left to 'fail'. One cannot help but feel that there is only limited further improvement to be achieved from the rather weary old nag that is the school system as we know it today.

# The need for a national strategy for learning

The ultimate and most fundamental question remains. Will our education system actually motivate and equip young people for life in the 21st century?

It is remarkable how little this question is asked of the activity in today's schools. While debates occasionally rage about the precise content of the national curriculum and some parents question the stress being put on children by the most heavily tested education system in the world, serious analysis of the dispositions and skills possessed by successful lifelong learners and the ways in which these might best be developed by schools has only just begun to reach the agenda.

What is needed, as the Campaign for Learning has already suggested, is a national strategy for learning that encompasses the full range of learning for the full range of life – from cradle to grave. Within this strategy, school improvement would be determined according to factors such as engagement with the community, parental involvement, staff morale and an emphasis on teaching and learning, quite as much as raising achievement in terms of grades. Pupils would understand that they must take responsibility for their own learning, that schooling involves learning for life in a variety of relevant contexts, and that education is primarily about understanding themselves as learners and how they can develop themselves.

In setting up the 'learning to learn' project our hypothesis has been that if such an approach could show a way of developing these skills and the teaching approaches required to support them, while simultaneously raising standards and the motivation of both groups, it might also help to inject some joy back into teaching.

# Building on firm foundations

The 'learning to learn' project has been able to draw and build on a wealth of thinking and practice already underway. In addition to working with the project schools and members of the advisory board (listed on page 8), it has developed thinking and partnerships with a range of bodies, including the DfES Standards and Effectiveness Unit, the RSA, the Lifelong Learning Foundation, the Design Council, Demos, universities – the Open University, Bristol and De Monfort – and a number of LEAs.

There are some encouraging signs. The unprecedented emphasis on teachers' professional development, particularly through the National Literacy and Numeracy Strategies, has established an excellent body of good practice and experience, much of which draws on research into the brain and how we learn. With the extension of these initiatives into secondary schools from September 2001 and, crucially, the launch of the Teaching and Learning in Foundation Subjects (TLF) strand of the Key Stage 3 strategy from September 2002, this work has already been consolidated. The TLF strand has been strongly influenced by research into assessment for learning and thinking skills and will seek to integrate this into the practice of teachers across Key Stage 3.

Other key government sponsored initiatives include the University of the First Age, which applies 'learning to learn' approaches to out-of-school hours learning, and the gifted and talented strand of the Excellence in Cities programme, which has helped incorporate work on developing meta-cognitive thinking into the practice of those teachers involved. Also outside the classroom, the new ConneXions service is building on previous work on Records of Achievement and the ProFile to encourage pupils to reflect on the learning they do throughout their lives and the ways in which they could develop this.

Most importantly, individual schools and local authorities have pioneered new thinking on learning through a range of projects and initiatives too numerous to detail here. Often these have drawn on thinking and practice from overseas, Neuro-Linguistic Programming (NLP) and English as a Foreign Language (EFL) teaching, thinking from adult learning and workplace training and work with pupils with Special Educational Needs.

Other school-based projects have been supported by external institutions, such as Kings College, which developed the CASE and CAME programmes, or Newcastle University's Thinking Skills project. Research in this area is currently ongoing in a number of universities, with several projects funded through the Economic and Social Research Council's (ESRC) Teaching and Learning Programme.

Another major influence on teaching practice has been the work on accelerated learning by writers such as Alistair Smith and Colin Rose, which has introduced concepts such as visual, auditory and kinesthetic and Howard Gardner's multiple intelligences as well as considerations about the learning environment to a wide audience.

Equally important in terms of the 'learning to learn' project is the work of Professor Guy Claxton and others at the University of Bristol, who have begun to conceptualize the qualities of effective lifelong learners and to develop a tool to measure and track these through the ELLI (Effective Lifelong Learning Instrument) project. Other projects allied to the 'learning to learn' work include the RSA's Redefining the Curriculum project, which is working with a group of schools to evaluate the impact of a competence-led (rather than content-led) curriculum based, SHA's new

Education for the Future Initiative and the ongoing work of John Abbott and the 21st Century Learning Initiative.

The 'learning to learn' project has consciously drawn on these different strands as well as the findings emerging from cognitive neuroscience and evolutionary biology. It has aimed to explore and evaluate new approaches to teaching and learning in the context of the policy developments described above. By developing an action research project which has been driven by the very real needs, concerns and interests of teachers themselves, it has attempted to create replicable solutions for the real world of the 21st century.

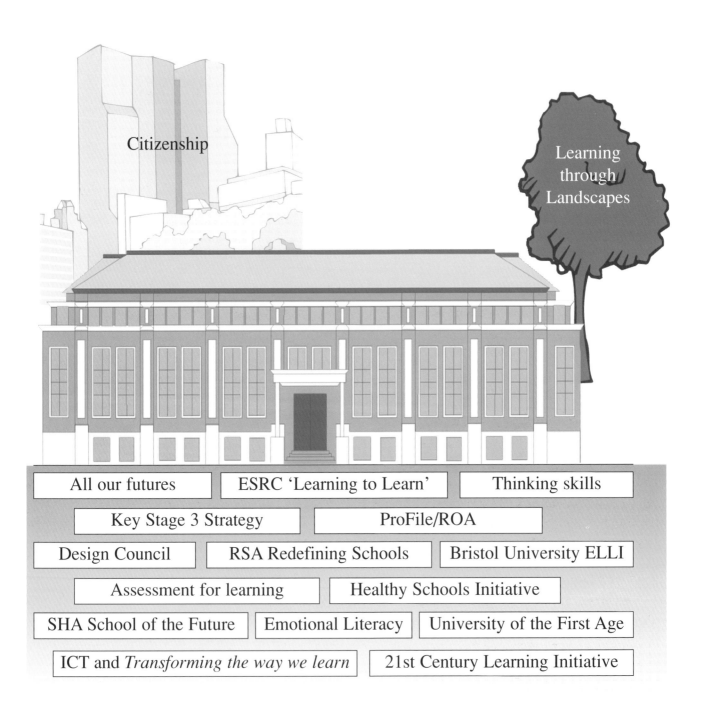

Citizenship

Learning through Landscapes

| All our futures | ESRC 'Learning to Learn' | Thinking skills |
|---|---|---|

| Key Stage 3 Strategy | ProFile/ROA |
|---|---|

| Design Council | RSA Redefining Schools | Bristol University ELLI |
|---|---|---|

| Assessment for learning | Healthy Schools Initiative |
|---|---|

| SHA School of the Future | Emotional Literacy | University of the First Age |
|---|---|---|

| ICT and *Transforming the way we learn* | 21st Century Learning Initiative |
|---|---|

# 3 | The 'learning to learn' research project and findings

## About the project

This report includes the findings from Phase 1 (September 2000 to July 2001) of the two-year 'learning to learn' project, which was originally set out in 'Learning to learn: Setting the agenda for schools in the 21st century'. Twenty-four schools throughout England and Wales were involved in this Phase, working with pupils from 3 to 18 years old. A separate Research Report published by the Campaign for Learning outlines the project's methodology and findings in more detail and is available on www.campaign-for-learning.org.uk. It is important to note that the findings from the research so far are interim findings and that a final report covering phases 1 and 2 of the project will be published in 2003.

The research was overseen by Dr Jill Rodd, an independent academic and educational consultant, and the project was co-ordinated by the Campaign for Learning. This team was supported by a high-level advisory board that included academics, practitioners and partner bodies (see page 8). The board met seven times over the course of Phase 1 to comment on the research design, implementation and evaluation.

Support for the schools was provided through four professional development training days and two residential workshops as well as through visits from members of the advisory board who acted as mentors. There was regular telephone, email and newsletter communication with the project team.

## About the project schools

The schools involved in the project were selected on the basis of research proposals designed and submitted by them. The 24 project schools chosen were selected from over 200 applications from interested schools and included 16 secondary schools and eight primary schools, including four that focused on Nursery and Reception pupils. Two schools were in Wales and the remainder were spread throughout England. The schools were:

Ashgate Nursery School, Derby, Derbyshire

Camborne School and Community College, Camborne, Cornwall

Campion School, Northamptonshire

Cornwallis School, Maidstone, Kent

Cramlington Community High School, Northumberland

Ellowes Hall School, Dudley

George Spencer School, Stapleford, Nottinghamshire

Henry Beaufort School, Winchester, Hampshire

Hipsburn First School, Lesbury, Northumberland

Kingdown School, Warminster, Wiltshire

King James's School, Knaresborough, North Yorkshire

Ladysmith First School, Exeter, Devon

Lytham St Anne's High Technology College, Lancashire

Malet Lambert School, Hull

Mortimer Comprehensive School, Tyne and Wear

Ogmore School, Bridgend, South Wales

Prince William School, Peterborough

Sandwich Technology School, Sandwich, Kent

St John's CE Primary, Salford, Greater Manchester

Summerhill School, Kingswinford, West Midlands

Tapton School, Sheffield

Tasker Milward School, Haverfordwest, Pembrokeshire, Wales

West Grove Primary School, Southgate, London

Westwood Park Primary School, Salford, Greater Manchester

This list was deliberately selected as representative of the wider schools population. For example, it includes schools:

- In the bottom 5 per cent for Key Stage 1 results
- Where approximately one-third of pupils are on the special needs register
- Where one-third of pupils have an ethnic minority background
- Where significant numbers of pupils entered the school with a reading age below their chronological age.

At the same time, it also includes schools where most of the Year 1 class meet the Key Stage 1 assessment test a year ahead of schedule and schools where Beacon School status has been achieved.

# The focus of the national project

The 'learning to learn' school-based action research project was designed to explore whether, and if so how, different 'learning to learn' approaches can help raise standards and create confident and effective lifelong learners.

Other areas of interest included the impact of 'learning to learn' approaches on:

- Teacher effectiveness, professional development and motivation
- The development of pupils as independent learners
- The involvement of parents
- School culture.

The key research question underpinning the research was: How can we help pupils to learn most effectively and so give each one the best chance to achieve his or her full potential?

The hypothesis underlying the research – described more fully in the first section – was that learning is learnable and that, if done successfully, this has a measurable impact on standards and motivation to learn. Inevitably, it was recognized that without a longitudinal study it is impossible to draw any conclusions about the effects of 'learning to learn' on the development of lifelong learners.

case study

# Assessment of Learning Styles

## Campion School – Year 7

### Aim

To assess how an understanding of preferred learning style and intelligence profile can help pupils learn more effectively.

### Process

**Learning style (defined through visual, auditory, kinestaetic – VAK – preference)**

- A short tick list questionnaire was completed which identified whether the pupil was currently a predominantly visual, auditory or kinesthetic learner.

- Findings were discussed to enable pupils to understand in more detail the terms and their meaning.

- Findings were then validated by checking pupils' sensory preference in a variety of school-based situations, for example, spelling, remembering, sport, science and so on.

**Multiple intelligences (Gardner)**

- Working with a partner, pupils were encouraged to decide how many of eight given 'intelligences' particularly applied to them.

- Pupils were then asked to think of occasions when they had used the intelligences.

- In groups of 4/5, pupils created role plays that showed the different intelligences at work in the brain.

- Once a good understanding had been gained a questionnaire was completed asking what pupils enjoyed, were good at, could do, liked, and so on.

- The scores were plotted on a wheel with 8 quadrants to form a profile.

The assessment of learning styles was part of a programme where one lesson a week was dedicated to 'learning to learn'. Subsequent questionnaires revealed that 87 per cent of the pupils found these lessons useful.

Pupils reported that the increased understanding helped them with the range of studies.

Findings added weight to the need for teachers to ensure lesson planning contained ample opportunity for VAK learning.

## Learning points

- Learning and self-esteem are enhanced when pupils understand how they can use their different strengths to help their studies and in other areas of their lives.

- It helps pupils to understand why information is sometimes not easy to comprehend, but that different learning strategies can help overcome this.

- Teachers can greatly enhance pupils' learning by ensuring lessons reflect the range of learning styles.

# About the research process

In Phase 1 each school designed its own research project within an overarching framework developed by the Campaign for Learning. The schools were each given the mind map on page 11 and asked to identify specific areas for research within this that they would like to explore and which might cast light on the ways pupils learn. Research areas chosen are detailed below and in the case studies included throughout this publication.

The project adopted an action research methodology, whereby the teachers involved in the project worked with Dr Rodd and the Campaign team to:

1. Define their research hypothesis. For example, 'Do young children display more positive attitudes to learning and improved performance if their learning styles are taken into consideration by teachers?'

2. Develop an approach for how teachers will implement the research, for example, 'In which lessons?' 'What development will teachers need?' and so on.

3. Define indicators of success for measuring whether the hypothesis has been met, for example, 'What do we mean by "positive attitudes to learning" and to what extent should they change?' 'Do we need target and control groups to evaluate the difference that the L2L interventions make?'

4. Agree the data needed to measure the indicators of success, for example, pre/post questionnaires for pupils.

5. Implement their approach.

6. Gather the data and report on the project according to a standard format.

Action research was chosen as the most appropriate research methodology for the project given its ability to extract findings based in real life school contexts. It is a process which:

- Leads to cycles of questioning, answer seeking and reflection.

- Encourages open-mindedness and a willingness to seek out and take account of various views.

- Encourages commitment to and the valuing of work in schools and its improvement.

- Encourages responsibility for professional development in the short and longterm.

Obviously, everyone involved in the project is aware of the limitations of this approach and the issues involved in using an action research framework. For example, the teachers involved in developing the learning approach are not necessarily best placed to evaluate its success, not just because of the demands on their time to do their job, but also because of their potential subjectivity and the risk that findings cannot be generalized to other settings.

Nevertheless, we believe that the advantages of the approach have far outweighed the limitations, not least because the teachers themselves have become skilled in research techniques and many have completed postgraduate qualifications as a result. As findings emerge, it is our intention to test them in situations where controls can be in place for all aspects of any hypothesis.

# Collecting the evidence

As a baseline for the project, MORI was commissioned by the Campaign to survey over 2000 11–16-year-old pupils in February 2000 on a range of 'learning to learn' issues. This was repeated in 2002 and some of the results have been included on page 30. The full results from the 2000 survey are included in *Learning to learn: Setting the agenda for schools in the 21st century.*

As a way of measuring the impact of the different approaches across 20 of the 24 schools, a standard questionnaire was administered at the beginning and end of the school year. A majority of the schools identified target and comparison groups in order to evaluate the impact of their 'learning to learn' interventions: 2511 'target' pupils completed this in September–October 2000 as well as 1442 'control' pupils aged 5 to 16 in 14 of the schools. This process was repeated during May–July 2001.

Beyond this, individual schools decided what data were available and meaningful in terms of their specific project and school agenda. This included quantitative data, such as national curriculum tests and GCSE scores, reading and spelling ages, pre- and post-academic test scores, attitudinal and learning style surveys and attendance, exclusion and behaviour figures. Qualitative data were also collected, including Ofsted reports, pupil interviews, reflections in diaries and videotaped discussions.

The range of data collected was intended to provide evidence relating to:

- Changes in pupils' performance, attainment and motivation.

- Changes in pupils' understanding, attributes and attitudes.

- Changes in teachers' practice and effectiveness.

- Changes in parental and wider community involvement (where relevant).

# Key areas covered by schools

The key areas covered by the schools involved in the project can be summarized as:

## Understanding how we learn

Some projects evaluated the impact of creating more autonomous and effective learners by providing 'learning to learn' induction courses or ongoing induction sessions for pupils to explore how we learn and how they could 'learn to learn'.

## Learning styles and multiple intelligences

A number of schools monitored the emergence of preferred learning styles and multiple intelligences and/or helped pupils develop their preferred learning style/portfolio of intelligences. Many focused primarily on the preferred method of data input – VAK – in their interpretation of learning styles.

## Application of 'learning to learn' approaches in specific curriculum areas

Some schools explored the application of meta-cognitive skills in specific subject areas by teaching learners to reflect on and improve their performance.

## Pupils' learning strategies

A number of schools assessed the impact of developing a toolkit of 'learning to learn' techniques for pupils.

## Teaching and learning approaches

Some schools evaluated the effectiveness of different 'learning to learn' teaching strategies such as delivering information through visual, auditory and kinesthetic approaches, following a learning cycle in all planning frameworks and/or teaching to meet the needs of different intelligences.

## Learning environments

Some schools identified the nature of a learning-friendly environment such as creating low threat, high challenge learning opportunities, the use of ICT or the relative importance of nutrition, water or sleep and the use of posters with learning messages and other visual stimulus as part of classroom display.

## Involvement of wider school and parents

Many schools assessed the impact of methods for the wider involvement of staff and parents in supporting 'learning to learn' approaches, for example, through the use of parents' evenings and staff handbooks.

## Wider impact of learning

Many of the schools investigated aspects of the wider impact of 'learning to learn' on pupils' emotional intelligence, resilience, resourcefulness, remembering, reflectiveness, responsiveness and creativity and explored how these qualities might be enhanced.

# 4 | The research findings

The key findings from the school-based research are reported here in three sections:

**A**  Early years

**B**  Year 7

**C**  Years 8–11

This breakdown reflects the focus of the 'learning to learn' work in schools during Phase 1 (September 2000–July 2001). The specific findings from individual schools have been integrated here into broad and general indications regarding the impact of 'learning to learn'. They are presented on photocopiable pages for use in staff INSET sessions with the learning mats as outlined in the third section. At this early stage of the research, it is not possible to report any wholly conclusive or definitive answers.

# A Early years

Five schools evaluated the impact of 'learning to learn' approaches with children in foundation stage and Key Stage 1. These included Ashgate Nursery School, Hipsburn First School (see case study on page 21), Ladysmith First School, St John's CE Primary and West Grove Primary School (see case study on page 47). St John's also included Year 6 pupils in their project.

The teachers at these schools had a strong interest in understanding the ways adults and children learn best. Key hypotheses included a belief that children learn in different ways and that the basis of future independent and autonomous learning is founded in emotional intelligence. A common aim was to evaluate whether tailoring education to individual learning styles helps realize children's potential.

Key influences on thinking included writers such as Howard Gardner, John Holt, Trevor Hawse, Alistair Smith and Daniel Goleman, and their work on brain-based learning, learning styles, emotional well-being and the impact of environmental factors on learning. Several authors who argue that lasting and important attitudes to learning are shaped in the early years were also influential in the schools' research, for example Margaret Carr, Guy Claxton, Christopher Ball, Carol Dweck, Lillian Katz, Tina Bruce and Christine Pascal. In addition, the recent government changes in approaches to early years curriculum, that is, a curriculum planned around early learning goals and areas of experience as opposed to subjects, offered an appropriate context for investigating the impact of 'learning to learn' approaches with young children.

# Key research questions

Although each of the four schools designed their own specific research questions, the following research questions broadly summarize the focus of the research in the early years.

- Can preferred learning styles be identified in children aged between three and eight years?

- Do 'learning to learn' approaches have a positive impact on achievement and attainment in children aged between three and eight?

- Does this way of working have a positive impact on the quality of teaching, teacher morale and job satisfaction?

- Do parents perceive 'learning to learn' as positive?

As is expected in school-based research, all of the schools found that their research raised many more questions and provided the beginnings of insights rather than definitive answers.

While the teachers reported difficulties in identifying preferred learning styles in the complex arena of the classroom, the list opposite summarizes some of the evidence-based indications that emerged from the research.

# Research findings: early years

## Outcomes for pupils

- Learning styles as defined by preferred method of processing data – VAK – appear to emerge in a sequential order in young children: kinesthetic, visual then auditory (KVA, not VAK).

- Visual and kinesthetic learning styles appear to be more common than auditory in young children.

- Some children appear to have a preferred learning style while others seem to move comfortably between a range of learning styles.

- Some children often chose a range of activities and thus, in theory, displayed no particular preference for learning style.

- Some children always chose the same activities, which were overwhelmingly kinesthetic, suggesting that that they had a preferred kinesthetic learning style.

- Boys, but not all boys, often appeared to be more kinesthetic in their preferred learning style.

- Many successful children in school are kinesthetic learners and some academic strugglers are strongly auditory.

- During the course of a week, children often had fewer opportunities to learn kinesthetically, especially during literacy and numeracy sessions.

- The children generally displayed good levels of attentiveness, confidence, independence, enthusiasm for learning and liking for school.

# Research findings: early years

## Outcomes for teachers

❏   Teachers reported feeling more confident about, satisfied with and effective in their teaching.

❏   Teachers reported being more willing to try out new ideas and to be honest about their outcomes with each other.

❏   Teachers have become aware of the need for the continual use of a wide range of teaching strategies in order to motivate most of the children most of the time. One teacher described her motivation in her teaching and research as 'trying to find the spark for learning in all children'.

❏   Many teachers have enrolled in higher degree courses as a result of being engaged in the 'learning to learn' project.

❏   Some of the teachers reported that, as a result of being part of the 'learning to learn' project, they 'have become much more interested in children's ideas about how they learn as well as our own ideas as teachers'.

# Research findings: early years

## Outcomes for schools

❏ Working on the 'learning to learn' project has helped many teachers develop a more collaborative approach, learn from each other and from their mentors and reinforced the idea of the school as 'a learning community'.

❏ One school has been invited by the DfES to feature in a new training video on provision for gifted and talented children.

❏ One school reported that, since 'learning to learn' has been implemented in the school, an increased number of applications for pupil places have been received and there has been a high application rate for the new jobs that were advertised.

# Research findings: early years

## Outcomes for parents

❏ Parents reported a high degree of satisfaction with the learning opportunities that their children were being offered at school, particularly opportunities for creativity and independent thinking.

❏ Parents in one of the schools reported that they are starting to understand more about how their children learn and how they as parents can help them learn.

❏ Parents appear to value discussions about their own child's learning and can see the relevance of learning styles and multiple intelligence to their own learning. Many parents reported that they discuss issues about learning at home.

# Teacher morale and motivation

## West Grove Primary School – Years 1–3

### Aim

To gauge how using L2L strategies impact on teacher morale and job satisfaction.

### Process

Pupils

- Curriculum planned around early learning goals and HMI (Areas of Learning and Experience).
- Strategies used include, Brain Gym®, VAK, pulse learning (concentration then relaxation), fruit and water in classrooms, use of music, meditation, circle time and bubble time.
- All pupils and parents involved. Information for parents through fortnightly newsletters, information evenings and 'have a go sessions'.

Teachers

- All staff trained in use of 'learning to learn' strategies.
- Staff training on INSET days and staff meetings include discussions about learning.
- Influences include Tina Bruce (schemas), Alistair Smith (ALPS) and Howard Gardner (multiple intelligences).
- Development planning aims to add to teachers' repertoire of strategies, for example by introducing Neuro-Linguistic programming (NLP), mind mapping and self-assessment strategies for pupils.

### Outcomes

- High teacher morale – 'Working at the school felt right straight away', 'I've never been so inspired'.
- Teachers confident to try out new ideas and be honest about the outcomes with each other.
- Teachers engaged in study at masters and doctorate levels.
- High application rate for new jobs advertised.
- Interest from other schools locally and nationally in what the school is doing.
- Positive comments from teachers from Investors in People assessment – 'The school thinks further than education and considers the whole child'.
- A recent Ofsted report commented 'The teachers are trying to maximize children's potential by tailoring their education to their individual learning styles. The stated aim is to enable all pupils to achieve high standards of learning and to develop self-confidence, optimism, high self-esteem, respect for others, and the achievement of personal excellence'.

### Learning points

- Focusing teachers on the core purpose for which they first came into the classroom – that is, learning – re-ignites and/or sustains motivation.
- Providing structured development opportunities for teachers in a range of L2L strategies enhances their flexibility and ability to support pupils' learning needs.
- It is enjoyable and satisfying to teach in a way that relates to the way each pupil learns and gets the best response.
- Positive feedback from pupils and parents is proof that the strategies work and is highly motivating.

# B Year 7

Ten schools investigated the impact of introducing a variety of 'learning to learn' courses to Year 7 pupils. The schools involved in this research included Campion (see case study on page 37), Ellowes Hall, Kingdown, Malet Lambert (see case study on page 31), Mortimer Comprehensive, Ogmore, Sandwich, Summerhill, Tapton and Tasker Milward schools. The focus of the research tended to be around measuring changes in attitudes and behaviour related to learning effectiveness. Some schools included measures of attainment in their research.

The structure and delivery of 'learning to learn' courses varied in each school, ranging from a one or two day course, a course of six weekly lessons, a course of weekly lessons throughout the year or where the 'learning to learn' content was embedded in the delivery of other subjects such as English, RE, PSHE and ICT. The approaches, skills and strategies were taught both explicitly and more subtly, for example, by arranging the classroom learning environment on the basis of 'learning to learn' principles and by displaying key messages about learning throughout the school environment.

The main areas of 'learning to learn' that were evaluated included brain-friendly learning, target-setting and affirmations, multiple intelligence learning, learning styles, memory techniques, thinking skills, mind mapping and creativity. One school evaluated an anger management course for certain pupils who had issues around dealing with anger.

The 'learning to learn' courses that were developed were underpinned by a range of philosophical and theoretical sources including leading work in:

- Cognitive neuroscience and thinking skills, including Maclean, Sperry, Buzan, Piaget, Vygotsky, Feuerstein

- Learning and intelligence, including Gardner, Claxton, Hughes, Lucas, Ginnis, Abbott, Powell

- Accelerated learning, including Rose, Smith

- Motivational psychology, including Lou Tice (The Pacific Institute), Deming

- Emotional intelligence and emotional literacy by Goleman.

Other influential authors included Carol McGuinness, Paul Black, Dylan Wiliam, Maurice Galton, John Gray and Jean Ruddock.

Each of the schools developed their own specific research questions that were focused upon putting learning back on the agenda in schools and embedding it in school culture.

# Key research questions

These were the range of research questions used with Year 7 pupils:

- Does participation in a 'learning to learn' course transform self-esteem and attitudes to learning and motivation in Year 7 pupils?

- Does participation in a 'learning to learn' course result in increased knowledgeability about the learning process and intelligence in Year 7 pupils?

- Does participation in a 'learning to learn' course increase understanding about the need for versatility in the use of learning styles in Year 7 pupils?

- Does participation in a 'learning to learn' course increase pupils' responsibility for their own learning?

- Does participation in a 'learning to learn' course have a positive impact on raising standards of attainment?

- Do teachers develop more positive perceptions and attitudes to teaching and learning as a result of using teaching strategies underpinned by 'learning to learn' principles?

- How can parents' understanding of 'learning to learn' approaches be developed so that they can help their children learn?

The following pages summarize some of the evidence that emerged from the research into Year 7 pupils' participation in 'learning to learn' courses.

# Research findings: Year 7

## Outcomes for pupils

❏   The vast majority of pupils gave positive feedback in terms of increased enjoyment of and fun in lessons.

❏   Brain Gym® and mind mapping consistently received positive responses from pupils.

❏   Pupils reported that understanding their learning style was useful for knowing how to learn best for a range of tasks and in a range of conditions.

❏   The overwhelming majority of pupils reported being very confident about their preparedness for learning, their ability to set learning goals and themselves as learners.

❏   Slightly more girls (approximately 5 per cent more than boys overall) were positive about the impact on their self-image as learners, self-esteem, self-confidence, preparation and strategies for learning.

❏   Group-work was perceived by many pupils to meet their needs because it encouraged support and sharing.

❏   Some pupils have begun to see opportunities for transfer across the curriculum.

❏   Some pupils reported that they would want some form of continuity into Year 8 and beyond through the timetable or in a cross-curricular day.

❏   Quantitative findings from some schools based on national curriculum tests and CAT scores revealed significant differences between the performance of target and comparison group pupils, with the level of target group pupils markedly higher in English, mathematics and science.

❏   Gender differences noted in data from some of the schools suggest that girls are happier at school and more positive about school, more willing to talk about feelings and seem to prefer to learn by listening. Boys appear to learn more by working in groups and on computers.

# Research findings: Year 7

## Outcomes for teachers

❏ Most teachers reported positive attitudes about the use of teaching strategies based on 'learning to learn' principles despite perceived increased demand in time for preparation and class management.

❏ 'Learning to learn' courses have contributed to wider input into developing teaching and learning across the curriculum.

❏ One school has developed a programme of departmental planning and support for accelerated learning.

❏ Some teachers reported that they now had higher expectations for the work produced by some of the pupils.

❏ Many teachers are completing a higher degree on the basis of their research into 'learning to learn'.

# Research findings: Year 7

## Outcomes for schools

❏ 'Learning to learn' has become embedded as part of the curriculum in most of the schools with some schools reporting that their School Development Plans are taking 'learning to learn' and accelerated learning into a range of subject areas.

❏ Some schools reported that pupils from other years want to have the opportunity to be involved with the 'learning to learn' curriculum.

❏ Evidence uncovers changing attitudes to teaching and learning throughout most schools.

❏ Some schools report that more staff are asking questions about and becoming interested in 'learning to learn' principles and practice.

❏ Some student teachers on School Experience have demonstrated an interest in 'learning to learn' and would like it incorporated in their training.

# Research findings: Year 7

## Outcomes for parents

❏ Some parents reported noticing a difference in their children's attitudes to learning, commenting that the children seemed to find learning more fun, they understood how they learned, how they wanted to be taught and what made learning effective.

❏ Those parents who had the opportunity to attend a parent workshop reported feeling more equipped with strategies to support their children's learning. Some parents reported finding the information of benefit to them personally.

## C Years 8–11

Seven schools investigated the impact of a range of 'learning to learn' approaches with pupils in Years 8, 9, 10 and 11 including King James's (Year 8), Cornwallis (Year 9), Camborne (Year 11 – see case study on page 27), Lytham St Anne's (Year 10), Prince William (Years 10 and 11) and George Spencer (Year 11). Cramlington investigated the impact of implementing the Accelerated Learning Cycle as a planning tool throughout the school, with an emphasis on Years 10 and 11 (see case study below). The focus of the research outcomes in these years tended to be on measurable improvement in attainment. However, evidence that identified improvements in attitudes and behaviour was also included.

The 'learning to learn' projects for pupils in Years 8 to 11 were underpinned by theories and ideas from writers including Buzan, Caine, Costa, de Bono, Feuerstein, Gardner, Goleman, Hannaford, Hughes, Jensen, Lipman, Smith and Vygotsky.

Many schools developed different types and styles of courses that trained pupils in a variety of thinking skills. Training pupils to use thinking skills in a range of curriculum areas, for example English, mathematics, science, history and geography, was a key focus of the research in Years 8 to 11. CAME and CASE courses were implemented in a couple of schools. A group of pupils from one school participated in a modern foreign language project in which an immersion method of language learning was used. One project explored the effects of teaching poetry to a mixed ability group of Year 8 pupils using a kinesthetic teaching and learning framework (see case study on page 18).

case study

## Accelerated learning cycle as a planning tool for lessons

### Cramlington Community High School – Years 9, 10, 11

Aim

To assess the results of using an accelerated learning planning tool for lessons.

Process

Lessons for Year groups planned using a six-step accelerated learning 'cycle' –MASTER– influenced by the thinking of Colin Rose, so that where possible every lesson would incorporate the following stages:

1. **Motivating the mind**

   Create relaxed, energized environment (music, Brain Gym®).

   Provide Big Picture context.

   Objectives clearly stated and shared.

2. **Acquiring information**

   Introduce material using learning preferences – visual, auditory and kinesthetic.

3. **Search out meaning**

   Help commit to 'permanent' memory by exploring material to bring to a level of real understanding.

4. **Triggering the memory**

   Short learning sessions (max 15 minutes) with plenty of beginnings and endings.

   Create multisensory memories.

   Use of mind maps/metaphors/grids/flow carts/flashcards/spider diagrams.

5. **Exhibit (practise) what has been learned**

   Apply/use understanding.

   Buddies, groups, parents, mentors.

   Role play, written assignments.

6. **Reflect (teachers and pupils)**

   What went well?

   What could have gone better?

   How can I improve for next time?

## Outcomes

- Attainment raised: 64 per cent of GCSE pupils achieved A-C grades up from 46 per cent the previous Year.

- Pupils report increased interest in lessons and understanding.

- OFsted report commented that 'teaching is characterized by a focus on well-structured planning, pace and challenge. Pupils are made to think.'

## Learning points

- Accelerated learning as part of a strategy for brain-based learning works at both a motivational and an attainment level.

- Teaching is more fun for pupils and teachers when multisensory approaches are taken.

- Providing a consistent structure as a planning tool helps teachers embed new thinking into their practice.

# Key research questions

The following research questions were used by schools working within Key Stage 3:

- Does the use of a preferred learning style enhance learning in Year 8 pupils?

- Does training in thinking skills provide a more personal learning experience for Year 8, 10 and 11 pupils?

- Does training in thinking skills improve learning effectiveness across all levels of ability?

- Are motivation and attainment rates in formal assessment raised where Year 11 pupils understand their preferred learning skills and are taught using multiple intelligence theory?

- Does a mentoring/coaching programme based on theories of multiple intelligence, preferred learning style and Neuro-Linguistic Programming have a significant impact on pupil achievement?

- Does the implementation of the Accelerated Learning Cycle as a planning tool in a 13 to 18 high school improve learning and raise standards in pupils?

Data about the impact of the use of accelerated learning and multiple intelligence theory in planning, teaching and assessment and training pupils in thinking skills in Years 8–11 generally reveal a positive impact on performance and other measures.

In some schools, marked differences were identified between the examination performance of target and comparison groups of pupils, with target group pupils demonstrating improved performance in a range of areas, including higher levels of thinking skills.

# Research findings: Years 8–11

## Outcomes for pupils

❏ The attainment of pupils with a kinesthetic learning style preference improved when teaching style complemented their learning style.

❏ Training in thinking skills appears to develop pupils' capacity to absorb, store, transfer and apply information to real world situations throughout the range of ability levels.

❏ Training in thinking skills appeared to provide a more holistic and enjoyable learning experience for pupils, catering for many different learning preferences and intelligences, including emotional intelligence.

❏ Training in thinking skills appeared to raise pupils' levels of motivation, confidence, self-esteem and involvement in learning.

❏ The majority of pupils considered that they have learned new skills and knowledge that will help them in future learning.

❏ Some pupils reported feeling more in control of their learning.

❏ A mentoring programme for Year 11 pupils appeared to raise motivation and achievement in many but not all pupils.

# Research findings: Years 8–11

## Outcomes for teachers

❏ Although some teachers reported concern about maintaining order and increased noise levels during lessons, the general consensus was positive and in favour of the principles and intentions underpinning the training and courses in thinking skills.

❏ Many teachers reported being more prepared to relinquish control, more comfortable about making mistakes and feeling more professionally aware.

❏ Some teachers reported that they needed extra support in classes where practical activities were being undertaken and where pupils had freedom to move around the room.

❏ Group sizes need to be kept small where practical work is involved.

❏ In some schools, teachers have formed working groups to discuss 'learning to learn' courses, resulting in a more coherent approach to the implementation of initiatives.

❏ Many teachers are using a wider range of resources in their teaching.

❏ Growing numbers of teachers in the schools support and actively implement brain-based teaching and learning strategies.

❏ Many teachers are undertaking higher degrees and focusing this research around 'learning to learn' issues.

# Research findings: Years 8–11

## Outcomes for schools

❏ Significant overall improvement in the class environment and learning has been noted in some schools.

❏ Levels of co-operation between pupils and teachers have increased in some schools.

❏ For some schools, allowing pupils freedom to choose their options was not viable on curriculum and timetabling grounds.

❏ Although a mentoring programme had a positive impact on pupil attitude and performance, there are massive time, cost and quality assurance implications.

❏ The quality of mentors and content of mentoring sessions are key factors in the success of a mentoring programme.

❏ 'Learning to learn' courses have been embedded in some schools, selected departments and some curriculum areas.

# Research findings: Years 8–11

## Outcomes for parents

While the majority of schools acknowledged the importance of involving parents in their research, no data regarding parent outcomes were reported. Many schools made reference to the need for involving parents in Phase 2 of the research project.

# The value of 'learning to learn'

While it is far too early to be able to make conclusive statements regarding the impact of 'learning to learn' approaches, the following section highlights the evidence available so far against some of the key indicators of success identified by the project team for the research.

## Can 'learning to learn' raise standards?

Many of the schools reported that it was impossible to make a judgement about the impact of 'learning to learn' on achievement and attainment. However, a number of those working in Year 7 and above reported improvements in standards. For example, evidence reported by different schools showed improved results in:

- English structured reading and science progress scores for Year 7 pupils,

- An increase of 5 per cent in one school's CSI.

- Increased average gains in Year 7 target group pupils' pre and post national curriculum tests and CAT scores for English, science and mathematics when matched against their comparison group pupil scores.

In one school, a target group of Year 9 pupils that had been exposed to a range of 'learning to learn' strategies consistently performed better in a range of tests relative to the comparison group, which was matched on academic ability. In addition, the target group showed greater improvement in academic tests from a baseline test, while the performance of some pupils in the comparison group decreased from the baseline. Although the differences were not statistically significant, they suggest that, over a longer period of time, pupils who understand some 'learning to learn' principles and strategies may perform better on academic tests than those who do not.

The majority of schools where 'learning to learn' was introduced to GCSE pupils reported improvements in GCSE results. In one school, 50 per cent of the pupils exceeded their predicted grades. In another school, the number of students achieving A–C grades in Key Stage 4 increased by 18 per cent when the 1999 and 2000 results were compared.

One school reported statistically significant differences between the results of the target group and comparison group of GCSE pupils. The target group that had participated in a multiple intelligence programme out performed the comparison group on a number of tests.

One school reported that the use of VAK approaches and the Accelerated Learning Cycle contributed to an improvement in the quality of teaching as judged by Ofsted inspectors.

## Can 'learning to learn' promote independent learning in pupils?

Many schools, especially those that implemented Year 7 'learning to learn' courses, reported the effectiveness of Brain Gym®, mind mapping, preferred learning styles (VAK) and accelerated learning techniques, such as giving pupils the Big Picture, sharing objectives and focusing on learning intentions and outcomes.

Many pupils reported that understanding their preferred learning style (VAK) and the concept of multiple intelligence helped them choose better strategies that enabled them to be successful in learning tasks. Knowing about their preferred learning style seemed to assist pupils to focus more on their schoolwork and become more motivated.

One group of pupils who were losing a football match decided to use Brain Gym® to improve their performance in the second half!

## Can 'learning to learn' help increase teachers' professional confidence and abilities?

Considerable evidence was reported from many schools concerning growing confidence and self-esteem in teachers as a result of their involvement in 'learning to learn'. Many teachers reported feeling that they could use their creativity and as a result enjoyed their work more. Involvement in 'learning to learn' appears to give teachers the confidence to try out new ideas and be honest about the outcomes with each other.

Higher levels of teacher motivation appear to be associated with teachers who incorporate 'learning to learn' principles, strategies and approaches into their teaching.

Many of the teachers involved in 'learning to learn' have focused their continuing professional development and training around issues related to this approach. A significant number of teachers are completing higher degrees and most of the teachers have attended numerous conferences, workshops and seminars to improve their knowledge and skills in 'learning to learn'. Many of these are in addition to the professional development days offered by the Campaign for Learning. Being a part of this project has had a vital impact on raising the professional development of participating teachers as well as raising awareness and stimulating enquiry in teachers who are not directly involved in the project.

A number of the teachers have been successful in obtaining DfES Best Practice Research Scholarships for 2001–2002. The funding, of up to £2,500, will be used to continue and extend their research into 'learning to learn'.

At least two of the teachers involved in the project have written books and produced video and CD-ROM resources about their practical experience of implementing 'learning to learn' in schools.

# Emerging conclusions

It is clear that a body of evidence is being amassed by the participating schools which indicates that the implementation of 'learning to learn' approaches in schools can

- Help develop positive dispositions to learning from the youngest pupils through to those who are completing their formal schooling.

- Encourage pupils to adopt flexible approaches to learning tasks that will increase the likelihood of success.

- Improve pupil and teacher motivation.

- Encourage the creation of learning environments both in classrooms and public spaces in schools that promote positive attitudes, behaviours and skills related to learning effectiveness.

Teaching pupils how to learn – *research, practice and INSET resources*

# 5 | Emerging issues for 'learning to learn' in schools

Phase 1 of the 'learning to learn' project has been a stimulating learning process for all those involved. Inevitably, the project has unearthed more questions than answers and these have formed the hypotheses for further research in Phase 2 for many of the schools involved. Issues highlighted from Phase 1 include:

## Early years and primaries

Definitive patterns regarding preferred learning styles (focusing on data-input) for children aged between three and eight years have still to be uncovered, but the initial indication that preferences follow sequentially K, then V, then A, is potentially huge and deserves further study.

Additional questions being investigated by the schools include:

- Do individual teachers define learning styles in different ways?

- Do children choose activities to be with particular friends rather than because of a preferred learning style?

- Do children who are taught to use self-assessment strategies learn more effectively?

- What teaching strategies help children learn more effectively?

- How can teachers encourage young children to develop positive dispositions to learning?

## Secondaries

Key issues to be explored and addressed in Phase 2 include:

- Time is needed to plan, test, evaluate and improve Year 7 'learning to learn' courses in schools, especially given the expanding information in the area.

- How can the Year 7 'learning to learn' courses be developed into the Year 8 curriculum?

- More research is needed to address unanswered questions about VAK, for example, VAK diagnoses and how to include VAK in lesson plans and schemes of work.

- The implications and impact of extending a mentoring programme and the Accelerated Learning Cycle to other Year groups need to be examined.

Although the general impact of 'learning to learn' courses for Year 7 pupils was evaluated as having very positive outcomes in terms of learning effectiveness, some concerns were raised by teachers. Some found that employing kinesthetic activities resulted in additional noise and disruption to classroom 'order', that furniture layout and space can present difficulties and that it can be more difficult to keep to times. Visual teaching was considered by some teachers to require considerable time for the preparation of materials. Auditory exercises tended to be predominantly teacher-centred and, regardless of how brief this was, it was considered to be 'the boring part of the lesson' by many pupils.

Building rapport with pupils and building pupil self-esteem take time and both processes are perceived by teachers to be vital to the success of such courses.

# Issues for further research

Lively debates took place throughout the year on a range of issues around 'learning to learn'. Can neuroscience really tell us anything useful yet in terms of actual classroom practice? If so what? What is the role of schools themselves as learning organizations in promoting 'learning to learn'? How and where should 'learning to learn' be integrated in an already busy curriculum? Is it possible to e-learn to learn?

One particularly interesting debate has been around learning styles. Many teachers reported that defining activities as visual, auditory or kinesthetic in order to assess learning style is problematic. The VAK classification reveals how learners might prefer to input and process information but does not necessarily offer insight into other aspects of learning processes or deeper personality traits. There are behaviourist methods already in existence, such as Honey and Mumford, or Yungian approaches, such as Myers Briggs.

Overly simplistic definitions of learning styles may be unhelpful and may simply re-categorize pupils according to new pigeonholes. More work clearly needs to be done in order to develop a useful diagnostic language of learning styles which will help learners to broaden their repertoire and teachers to plan interventions accordingly.

Other issues relate to school cultures and structures. While support from the headteacher and strong staff commitment and training are clearly essential, the subtle influences on learning culture within a school are not yet understood.

What seems clear is that at every stage, more work is needed on:

- Gender differences and 'learning to learn'.
- The impact of 'learning to learn' courses on standards.
- Transferability between subjects, 'real life' situations and stages and how to involve parents and teaching assistants.
- The role of 'learning to learn' approaches in developing lifelong learning dispositions and abilities.

# Emerging recommendations

Nevertheless, the campaign has been able to make the following recommendations based on the findings to date:

Given the potential impact of 'learning to learn' on teacher morale and motivation:

*Initial training and ongoing career development for teachers and school support staff should include modules and structured research opportunities on how humans learn and the factors that promote and inhibit effective learning. This should initially be piloted through a minimum of three ITT institutions and the schools in three Local Education Authorities.*

Given the potential impact of 'learning to learn' on pupil standards and motivation:

*Teachers should be supported with curriculum time and resources to help pupils take responsibility for their own learning by helping them understand the process of learning and themselves as learners.*

*Teachers should be helped to utilize 'learning to learn' principles and practices for pupils of all ages in terms of how they structure the learning environment, deliver information, facilitate learning opportunities and provide formative feedback.*

*Teachers should be assessed on their competence in utilizing 'learning to learn' approaches.*

*Parents should be offered opportunities to understand learning so that they can effectively support their children's learning.*

These proposals have a number of practical resource and policy implications, including the following:

'Learning to learn' should be seen as a central plank in the shift towards more individualized teaching approaches and should involve teaching assistants and new technologies as appropriate.

'Learning to learn' should be embedded within schools and Local Education Authorities through its explicit inclusion in School and Local Education Authority Development Plans.

'Learning to learn' Specialist and Beacon schools should be established as a means of furthering our understanding in this area and spreading good practice.

The Effective Teaching and Learning component of the Key Stage 3 strategy should reflect the project's findings and should allocate curriculum time and resources to support their implementation.

Further research should be undertaken into the impact of new approaches to teaching and learning, conducted by teachers, academics and researchers with rigorous controls and ideally longitudinally.

# Content of Phase 2 research

18 schools are participating in Phase 2 of the project in the following areas.

## Ashgate Nursery School
Derbyshire, Nursery

Using a child's preferred learning style to encourage development in curriculum areas that the child may choose to ignore.

The use of multiple intelligence record sheets to monitor progress from Nursery throughout school career.

The effect of using a parents/carers and children learning group on the motivation to learn.

## Camborne School and Community College
Cornwall, 11-18 Mixed Comprehensive

Measuring the effectiveness of the application of multiple intelligence strategies on teaching and learning.

The impact on learning of 'positiveness' gained through self-talk. The process to be supported by mentoring.

## Campion School
Northampton, 11–18 Mixed Comprehensive

Application of L2L thinking skills on extended range of curriculum subjects.

Teacher techniques including NLP responding to feedback from L2L: findings in Phase 1.

## Christ Church School
Wiltshire, Primary

Measuring the impact of learning strategies for developing the 3 Rs at Key Stage 2 on individual children's perception of themselves as learners and on their attitude to learning.

## Cornwallis School
Kent, 11–18 Mixed Comprehensive

Teacher perceptions on impact of L2L across extended range of teachers and departments.

Linking L2L feedback to pupil attainment and attendance.

## Cramlington Community High School

Northumberland, 11–18 Mixed Comprehensive

Student self-assessment of learning.

## Ellowes Hall School

West Midlands, 11–18 Mixed Comprehensive

Evaluating the impact of parents, learning support assistants and learning co-ordinators on standards of attainment.

Impact of VAK strategies on science curriculum.

## Hipsburn County First School

Northumberland, First School

Impact of motivation/self-esteem on learning and expectations of attainment.

Impact of parental involvement on 'learning to learn'.

## Kingdown School

Wiltshire, 11–18 Mixed Comprehensive

Impact on confidence on learning of L2L curriculum.

The time of a lesson and the school day as an influence on the ability to learn.

The impact of the physical environment on the ability to learn.

## Ladysmith First School

Devon, First School

Identifying children's disposition to learning.

Impact of implementation of brain-friendly teaching styles on Key Stage 1 and Key Stage 2 children.

Evaluation of learning stories as an indicator of learning and learning preferences.

## Lytham St Anne's High School

Lancashire, 11–18 Mixed Comprehensive

Teachers' attitude to change and the impact on learning.

Modelling as a strategy for improving learning.

### Malet Lambert School
Hull, 11–18 Mixed Comprehensive

The impact of a structured programme of thinking skills on the acceleration of the learning process and the impact on motivation.

### Mortimer Comprehensive School
Tyne and Wear, 11–16 Mixed Comprehensive

Wider development of L2L skills into extended range of subjects.

Parental involvement in L2L.

### Ogmore School
South Wales, 11–18 Mixed Comprehensive

Evaluating strategies for building confidence and autonomous learning in pupils.

The teacher's role in supporting autonomous learning and the impact on teacher and pupil performance.

### Prince William School
Northamptonshire, 13–18 Mixed Comprehensive Upper

Using Suggestopedia for language learning.

Multiple intelligences as a key to understanding and accessing appropriate learning.

### Sandwich Technology School
Kent, 11–18 Mixed Comprehensive

The impact of pupil mentors on learning and motivation.

### Summerhill School
West Midlands, 11–16 Mixed Comprehensive

The classroom of the future and the impact on learning.

### West Grove Primary School
London, Primary

Whole-school approach to learning involving parents, a child-centred curriculum and a learning environment incorporating water, fruit and music as a background to activities.

# 6 | Putting 'learning to learn' into practice in your school

Do you agree with the theory of 'learning to learn', outlined in the first section of *Teaching pupils how to learn*? Or does the experience of the schools in the research project ring true to you? If so, you may want to develop similar approaches in your school.

To help you do this we have included two learning mats with this publication to help you to structure a dialogue with your colleagues. We imagine that you will want to explore these issues in your school to establish what people think before formulating any plans.

In this section you will find suggestions for using the learning mats as part of your school's in-service training programme. Each mat has the potential to stimulate work lasting as little as an hour or as long as a whole day. You can obtain more copies of the mats from Network Educational Press. Learning mats work best when those using them are sitting around small tables of about five people.

For each mat there are guidance notes indicating how you might use them. These have been written to help whoever is facilitating the discussions, but could also be used to guide self-study. We have also suggested other activities which might precede, extend or follow those suggested on the mats themselves.

Then there is a list of more general questions which you may find helpful, followed by some quotations to get you thinking.

And finally there is a list of resources to help you. You might also like to photocopy the research findings from the 'learning to learn' project as a way of stimulating debate around the mats. Of course, one of the best ways of introducing change is to visit a school that has done something similar or is thinking about doing so. Case studies on the ALITE web site – alite.co.uk – can help you do this. Or you might want to look at the online 'learning to learn' course – learntolearn.org – developed with accelerated learning expert, Colin Rose.

# Learning mat 1

### 'Learning to learn' in schools: taking stock

As its title suggests, the aim of this mat it to help you carry out a health check on the state of learning in your school. It has also been designed to ensure that the different views about learning that will inevitably exist in any staffroom will be aired.

## Before you start

Give advance warning of the session. Encourage colleagues to bring in press cuttings, children's work or any other material that they think may stimulate debate about the state of learning in your school.

## Setting the scene

Explain that you are going to do a health check on the state of learning in the school and that you are going to use the learning mat to structure discussion about this. Encourage colleagues to write on the mats and to be creative about adding materials or techniques that they wish to contribute. Stress that much of learning theory is common sense and intuitive, but nevertheless encourage your colleagues to expect to learn something new!

## Using the mat

### 1. Have we got it right today?

Use this part of the session to flush out both the positive and negative factors affecting schools today. Try not to get drawn into any one particular area, especially if any colleague has a well-known hobby horse! Ensure that discussion goes beyond your own school and explores the broader horizon. You might like to capture the discussion on flip charts or use Blu-tack to pin up any images brought in.

### 2. What has changed in the last twenty years?

For those not familiar with the mind map concept, introduce it here. This section falls into two halves. The first looks at the Big Picture, the second at the world of school. Use the mind maps as a means of structuring feedback. You could encourage different groups to report back on the aspect that has most engaged them.

### 3. What do you know about the mind and intelligence?

This can be a difficult section as, remarkably, teachers go through most of their initial training with little or no input in this area, apart from, say, something about Jean Piaget if they are lucky! Try to avoid making anyone feel stupid or ill-informed by anticipating the likelihood that they may not have much explicit knowledge. Once you start brainstorming, you will probably find that colleagues do, of course, know a huge amount about this area. You might like to have copies of some of the books listed on page 77 as follow-up material for those who would like it.

### 4. What is your model of the learning process?

Encourage colleagues to look at the stimulus material first. Then ask them to think of something they have learned recently, for example, how to use a new computer program, how to accept feedback, how to speak French and so on. Get them to think back to the different stages they went through before achieving competence.

Then suggest they try to draw their own process diagram on a separate piece of paper before trying to come up with a composite model for their group.

## Follow-up

Depending on the outcome of your discussions you might like to suggest that staff members

- Visit a school that is already doing 'learning to learn'
- Read some of the materials
- Invite an expert to run a further training session
- Attend a conference that explores 'learning to learn'
- Hold a similar session with parents or governors
- Go on to explore learning mat 2.

# Learning mat 2

### 'Learning to learn' in schools: moving on

## Before you start

Give advance warning of the session. If you are not holding it immediately after the one based on learning mat 1, then make sure you have explored learning mat 1, and that colleagues bring their memos.

## Setting the scene

Explain that the purpose of the session is to build on the one you did using learning mat 1 and see what, if anything, staff would like to focus on and do differently. Suggest that you are open as to whether any change is small and experimental, for example, one class trying something, or more holistic, for example, a whole Year group undertaking a systematic 'learning to learn' course with all subject specialists (if at Secondary level) adapting their lesson planning accordingly.

## Using the mat

There are only two sections to this mat. The first is all about WHAT (taking stock) and the second deals with HOW (moving on). Teachers (as do all of us) have a tendency to want to rush from the what to the how before they have really settled on what it is and why they want to do it! So use this structure to your benefit as a facilitator. Say things like: 'Don't worry about how you are going to make it happen, just focus on what it is you want to do. The how can wait!'

### Section 1

After you have shared the memos, capture any key points on a flip chart. If anyone finds it difficult to focus on WHAT they want to change, try prompting them with questions such as: 'So what would be different for pupils?' 'What would be different about the curriculum?'

### Section 2

Encourage your colleagues to use the blank chart to help them begin to think about how they will implement changes. Who, Why, Where, When questions are useful here.

If anyone gets stuck, suggest that they try

- Thinking of the opposite of what they have said so far
- Thinking what somebody else might think

anything to help them break out of their conventional thought processes.

If you encounter people who say 'We could not do this because…' or its many equivalent phrases, then hear them out, but refuse to be thrown off course. Put any such apparently insuperable problems on a piece of paper somewhere in the room and come back to them at the end.

You might like to try a technique called 'feedforward' to work on any outstanding issues. Take each one in turn and ask the whole group to go into problem-solving mode. Get them to use this formula 'You might like to….' to introduce possible solutions. The great thing about this technique is that it encourages positive thinking and ownership of problems and discourages isolated cynics!

The output of this session and the whole learning mat process is for staff to be clearer about what they want to change and how they want to change things. Some people do not like the flow chart approach, so be ready to encourage groups to come up with their own versions.

If your school has a method it like to use, then you may like to use that one.

## Follow-up

Once you get started on implementing changes, you will need lots of support.

As you start to plan, it is worth building in simple methods of checking on your progress. If you begin with the conclusion in mind, then you may be able to describe what success would look and feel like!

# Some questions to consider

During either of the learning mat sessions, or to stimulate dialogue as you move forward, you may find these questions useful in provoking thought:

Do you conduct attitudes to learning surveys among your pupils?

Are pupils confident as learners? How would you know this?

Does your school attempt to understand different learning styles? If so, how?

What strategies does the school have for encouraging pupils to become effective lifelong learners?

How often are pupils encouraged to reflect on their progress? How is this done?

How willing are pupils to try out new approaches?

Are pupils taught how to remember?

How confident are the staff? How do you know?

Do all staff have the opportunity to observe other colleagues teach?

Do staff consciously seek to model learning habits? If so, how?

Do all staff set out the objectives of each term's work to parents and to pupils in accessible language?

Do all teachers set out the objectives of each lesson to pupils before starting?

Do staff consciously seek to connect with the experience of their pupils?

How do staff reflect on their own teaching and learning?

Do staff teach pupils how to learn?

How confident are parents about coming in to school?

In what ways are parents involved as co-educators?

How does the school's policy on the display of pupil's work encourage learning?

Do you display other materials? If so, what and why?

# Some useful quotations

During either of the learning mat sessions, or to stimulate dialogue as you move forward, you may also find these quotations useful in provoking thought.

Do you agree with them? Do you disagree? What do they make you think?

*'Those who are going nowhere, usually get there'*

Henry Ford

*'Imagination is more important than knowledge'* and *'Our theories determine what we measure'*

Albert Einstein

*'Never let formal education get in the way of your learning'*

Mark Twain

*'The potential danger for schools lies in the privacy of the classroom'*

Charles Handy

*'The great thing, then, in all education, is to make our nervous system our ally instead of our enemy.'*

William James

'People who are only good with hammers see every problem as a nail'

Abraham Maslow

'The chief object of education is not to learn things but to unlearn things'

GK Chesterton

'The only real object of education is to leave a person in the condition of continually asking questions'

Tolstoy

'Learning to learn is the lifelong shadow of learning itself'

Guy Claxton

'Since we cannot know what knowledge will be most needed in the future, it is senseless to try to teach it in advance. Instead, we should try to turn out people who love learning so much and learn so well that they will be able to learn whatever needs to be learned.'

John Holt

'The longest distance is between an official state curriculum policy and what goes on in a child's mind'

Peter Schrang

'This is what learning is. You suddenly understand something you've understood all your life, but in a new way'

Doris Lessing

# 7 | Useful resources

## Useful books

John Abbott and Terry Ryan, *The unfinished revolution: learning, human behaviour, community and political paradox*, Network Educational Press, 2000

Jackie Beere, *The Key Stage 3 learning toolkit*, Connect Publications, 2002

Paul Black and Dylan Wiliam, *Inside the black box*, King's College London, 1998

Garry Burnett, *Learning to learn: making learning work for all students*, Crown House, 2002

Tony Buzan, *Use your head*, BBC Consumer Publishing, 2000

Renate Caine and Geoffrey Caine, *Unleashing the power of perceptual change*, ASCD, 1997

Rita Carter, *Mapping the mind*, Orion Fiction MMP, 2000

Guy Claxton, *Hare brain, tortoise mind*, Fourth Estate, 1998

Guy Claxton, *Wise up, the challenge of lifelong learning*, Network Educational Press, 2000

Howard Gardner, *Frames of mind; the theory of multiple intelligences*, Basic Books, 1993

Daniel Goleman, *Emotional intelligence; why it matters more than IQ*, Bloomsbury, 1996

Susan Greenfield, *Brain story*, BBC Consumer Publishing, 2000

Susan Greenfield, *The private life of the brain*, John Wiley & Sons, 2001

Carla Hannaford, *Smart moves, why learning is not all in your head*, Great Ocean Publishers, 1995

Peter Honey and Alan Mumford, *The learning styles questionnaires; 80 item version*, Peter Honey Publications, 2000

Mike Hughes, *Closing the learning gap*, Network Educational Press, 1999

Pierce Howard, *The owner's manual for the brain*, Bard Press, 2000

Anne Kite, *A guide to better thinking: positive, critical, creative*, nferNelson, 2000

Eric Jensen, *The learning brain*, The Brain Store Inc., 1995

Bill Lucas, *Power up your mind; learn faster, work smarter*, Nicholas Brealey Publishing, 2001

Bill Lucas and Toby Greany, *Schools in the learning age*, Southgate Publishers, 2000

Bill Lucas and Toby Greany, *Learning to learn: setting an agenda for schools in the 21st century*, Network Educational Press, 2001

Carol McGuiness, *From thinking skills to thinking classrooms*, DfES, 1999

National Research Council (US), *How people learn; brain, mind, experience and the classroom*, National Academy Press, 2000

Carl Rogers and Jerome Freiberg, *Freedom to learn*, Prentice Hall, 1994

Colin Rose and Malcolm Nicholl, *Accelerated learning for the 21st century*, Piatkus Books, 1997

Martin Seligman, *Learned optimism: how to change your mind and your life*, Pocket Books, 1998

Peter Senge et al., *Schools that learn*, Nicholas Brealey Publishing, 2000

Alistair Smith, *Accelerated learning in the classroom*, Network Educational Press, 1996

Alistair Smith, *Accelerated learning in practice*, Network Educational Press, 1998

Alistair Smith and Nicola Call, *The ALPS approach resource book*, Network Educational Press, 2001

*Transforming the way we learn: a vision for the future of ICT in schools*, DfES, 2002

Colin Weatherley, *Leading the learning school*, Network Educational Press, 2000

Derek Wise and Mark Lovatt, *Creating an accelerated learning school*, Network Educational Press, 2001

## Other resources

Assessment Reform Group, *Assessment for Learning*

Learning to learn in schools: Phase 1 project Research Report, Dr Jill Rodd (available from www.campaign-for-learning.org.uk)

Teaching and Learning Research Programme (ESRC) *Newsletters*

## Useful websites

alite.co.uk – Alistair Smith's accelerated learning site

campaign-for-learning.org uk – the Campaign for Learning's site

learntolearn.org – CHAMPS, the first online 'learning to learn' course developed by Accelerated Learning Systems with the Campaign

21learn.org – the 21st Century Learning Initiative site

networkpress.co.uk – Publishers of many 'learning to learn' books

accelerated-learning.co.uk – distributors of many 'learning to learn' books

ex.ac.uk/ESRC-TLRP/ – the ESRC Teaching and Learning Research Programme site

standards.dfes.gov.uk – the DfES Standards and Effectiveness Unit site, including the Teaching and Learning in Foundation Subjects (TLF) Key Stage 3 strand